1st Workshop on Natural Language Processing for Programming (NLP4Prog 2021)

Held online due to COVID-19

Bangkok, Thailand
6 August 2021

ISBN: 978-1-7138-3383-3

Printed from e-media with permission by:

Curran Associates, Inc.
57 Morehouse Lane
Red Hook, NY 12571

Some format issues inherent in the e-media version may also appear in this print version.

Association for Computational Linguistics
209 N. Eighth Street
Stroudsburg, Pennsylvania 18360

Phone: 1-570-476-8006
Fax: 1-570-476-0860

acl@aclweb.org

Additional copies of this publication are available from:

Curran Associates, Inc.
57 Morehouse Lane
Red Hook, NY 12571 USA
Phone: 845-758-0400
Fax: 845-758-2633
Email: curran@proceedings.com
Web: www.proceedings.com

NLP4Prog 2021

The 1st Workshop on Natural Language Processing for Programming (NLP4Prog 2021)

Proceedings of the Workshop

August 6, 2021
Bangkok, Thailand (online)

Message from the Organizers

Welcome to NLP4Prog, the First Workshop on Natural Language Processing for Programming, co-located with ACL-IJCNLP 2021 online.

The proliferation of programming-related platforms such as GitHub and Stack Overflow has led to large amounts of rich, open-source data consisting of programs associated with natural language, such as natural language questions and answers with code snippets, open-source repositories with natural language comments, and communications between software developers. At the same time, deep learning based techniques have shown promising performance for modeling both natural language and computer programs. Driven by these revolutions on data and models, recent years have witnessed a major resurgence of using NLP techniques to assist programming (NLP4Prog).

As promising as the current developments are, there are still many challenges remaining. This workshop aims to bring related communities (e.g., NLP, Software Engineering, Programming Language, Human-Machine Interaction, Robotics) together to review the recent advances related to NLP4Prog and discuss the remaining challenges and what to expect in the short- and long-term future. While there are similar workshops such as NLP-SEA and NLPaSE held recently, most of them are in conjunction with software engineering venues; to the best of our knowledge, this is the first workshop focusing on NLP for programming and to be held in NLP venues.

A total of 31 papers were submitted and 25 were presented at the workshop. 10 of these papers appear in the proceedings, while the rest were submitted under a non-archival option. In addition, 4 papers from Findings of ACL were also offered presentation slots.

We are thankful to all reviewers for their help in the selection of the program, for their readiness in engaging in thoughtful discussions about individual papers, and for providing valuable feedback to the authors. We would also like to thank the ACL workshop organizers for all the valuable help and support with organizational aspects of the conference. Finally, we would like to thank all our authors and presenters for making this such an exciting event!

NLP4Prog Organizers: Royi Lachmy, Ziyu Yao, Greg Durrett, Milos Gligoric, Junyi Jessy Li, Ray Mooney, Graham Neubig, Yu Su, Huan Sun, Reut Tsarfaty

Organizing Committee

- Royi Lachmy (Bar-Ilan University)
- Ziyu Yao (The Ohio State University)
- Greg Durrett (UT Austin)
- Milos Gligoric (UT Austin)
- Junyi Jessy Li (UT Austin)
- Ray Mooney (UT Austin)
- Graham Neubig (Carnegie Mellon University)
- Yu Su (The Ohio State University/Microsoft Semantic Machines)
- Huan Sun (The Ohio State University)
- Reut Tsarfaty (Bar-Ilan University)

Program Committee

- Miltos Allamanis (MSR, Cambridge)
- Uri Alon (Technion, Israel)
- Jonathan Berant (Tel Aviv University)
- Ben Bogin (Tel Aviv University)
- Saikat Chakraborty (Columbia University)
- Xinyun Chen (UC Berkeley)
- Hanjun Dai (Google Brain)
- Xiang Deng (The Ohio State University)
- Elizabeth Dinella (Univ. of Pennsylvania)
- Li Dong (Microsoft Research Asia)
- Ahmed Elgohary (University of Maryland)
- Xiaodong Gu (HKUST)
- Vincent J. Hellendoorn (CMU)
- Julia Hockenmaier (UIUC)
- Toby Jia-Jun Li (CMU)
- Omer Levy (Tel Aviv University, Israel)
- Victoria Lin (Salesforce)
- Jian-Guang Lou (Microsoft Research Asia)

- Pengyu Nie (UT Austin)
- Sheena Panthaplackel (UT Austin)
- Ice Pasupat (Google AI; Stanford)
- Kyle Richardson (AI2)
- Richard Shin (UC Berkeley)
- Alane Suhr (Cornell)
- Ronen Tamari (Hebrew university)
- Fangzheng (Frank) Xu (CMU)
- Xi Ye (UT Austin)
- Pengcheng Yin (CMU)
- Tao Yu (Yale)
- Rui Zhang (Penn State)
- Ruiqi Zhong (UC Berkeley)

Table of Contents

Conference Program

Friday August 6, 2021

10:05am EDT Session 1

10:05am *Code to Comment Translation: A Comparative Study on Model Effectiveness & Errors*
Junayed Mahmud, Fahim Faisal, Raihan Islam Arnob, Antonios Anastasopoulos and Kevin Moran

10:17am *ConTest: A Unit Test Completion Benchmark featuring Context*
Johannes Villmow, Jonas Depoix and Adrian Ulges

10:30am *CommitBERT: Commit Message Generation Using Pre-Trained Programming Language Model*
Tae Hwan Jung

10:30am *Time-Efficient Code Completion Model for the R Programming Language*
Artem Popov, Dmitrii Orekhov, Denis Litvinov, Nikolay Korolev and Gleb Morgachev

10:30am *CoTexT: Multi-task Learning with Code-Text Transformer*
Long Phan, Hieu Tran, Daniel Le, Hieu Nguyen, James Annibal, Alec Peltekian and Yanfang Ye

10:30am *DIRECT : A Transformer-based Model for Decompiled Identifier Renaming*
Vikram Nitin, Anthony Saieva, Baishakhi Ray and Gail Kaiser

4:15pm EDT Session 2

4:40pm *Shellcode_IA32: A Dataset for Automatic Shellcode Generation*
Pietro Liguori, Erfan Al-Hossami, Domenico Cotroneo, Roberto Natella, Bojan Cukic and Samira Shaikh

4:40pm *Reading StackOverflow Encourages Cheating: Adding Question Text Improves Extractive Code Generation*
Gabriel Orlanski and Alex Gittens

4:40pm *Text-to-SQL in the Wild: A Naturally-Occurring Dataset Based on Stack Exchange Data*
Moshe Hazoom, Vibhor Malik and Ben Bogin

4:40pm *Bag-of-Words Baselines for Semantic Code Search*
Xinyu Zhang, Ji Xin, Andrew Yates and Jimmy Lin

Friday August 6, 2021 (continued)

Code to Comment Translation: A Comparative Study on Model Effectiveness & Errors

Junayed Mahmud, Fahim Faisal, Raihan Islam Arnob, Antonios Anastasopoulos, Kevin Moran
Department of Computer Science
George Mason University, USA
jmahmud,ffaisal,rarnob,antonis,kpmoran@gmu.edu

Abstract

Automated source code summarization is a popular software engineering research topic wherein machine translation models are employed to "translate" code snippets into relevant natural language descriptions. Most evaluations of such models are conducted using automatic reference-based metrics. However, given the relatively large semantic gap between programming languages and natural language, we argue that this line of research would benefit from a qualitative investigation into the various error modes of current state-of-the-art models. Therefore, in this work, we perform both a quantitative and qualitative comparison of three recently proposed source code summarization models. In our quantitative evaluation, we compare the models based on the smoothed BLEU-4, METEOR, and ROUGE-L machine translation metrics, and in our qualitative evaluation, we perform a manual open-coding of the most common errors committed by the models when compared to ground truth captions. Our investigation reveals new insights into the relationship between metric-based performance and model prediction errors grounded in an empirically derived error taxonomy that can be used to drive future research efforts.[1]

1 Introduction and Motivation

Proper documentation is an important component of modern software development, and previous studies have illustrated its advantages for tasks ranging from program comprehension (Garousi et al., 2015) to software maintenance (Chen and Huang, 2009). However, manually documenting software is a tedious task (McBurney and McMillan, 2014) and modern agile development practices tend to champion working code over extensive documentation (Beck et al., 2001). As such, a range of important documentation activities are often neglected (Zhi et al., 2015) leading to deficiencies in carrying out development activities and contributing to technical debt. Because of this, researchers have worked to develop automated code summarization techniques wherein machine translation models are employed to generate precise, semantically accurate natural language descriptions of source code (Haiduc et al., 2010). Due to the promise and potential benefits of effective automated source code summarization techniques, this area of work has seen constant and growing attention at the intersection of the software engineering and natural language processing research communities (Zhu and Pan, 2019).

Various techniques for automated source code summarization have been explored extensively over the past decade. Some of the earliest approaches made use of a combination of structural code information and text retrieval techniques for determining the most relevant terms (Haiduc et al., 2010), with follow up work investigating the use of topic modeling (Eddy et al., 2013). Techniques then evolved from using information retrieval to canonical machine learning techniques, with Ying and Robillard (2013) using supervised Naive Bayes and Support Vector Machine classifiers to identify code fragment lines that could be used as suitable summaries. One of the first appearances of language modeling came from McBurney and McMillan (2016) who proposed an approach combining a software word usage model, natural language generation systems, and the PageRank algorithm (Langville and Meyer, 2006) to generate summaries. Driven by the advent of deep learning, current state-of-the-art techniques generally make use of large-scale neural models and have significantly improved the performance of code summa-

[1] Our annotations and guidelines are publicly available on Github https://github.com/SageSELab/CodeSumStudy and Zenodo: https://doi.org/10.5281/zenodo.4904024.

Proceedings of the 1st Workshop on Natural Language Processing for Programming (NLP4Prog 2021), pages 1–16
August 1–6, 2021.

rization tasks. For instance, Iyer et al. (2016) used Long Short Term Memory (Hochreiter and Schmidhuber, 1997) with attention (Bahdanau et al., 2015) to generate summaries from a code snippet. Following this work, researchers have applied several deep learning-based approaches to the task of source code summarization (Zhang et al., 2020a; Wan et al., 2018; LeClair et al., 2020).

In most works on automated code summarization, the performance of the generated natural language descriptions is evaluated using reference-based metrics adapted from machine translation, e.g., BLEU (Papineni et al., 2002) and METEOR (Lavie and Agarwal, 2007), or text summarization, e.g., ROUGE (Lin, 2004). As such, most researchers make conclusions based on the results obtained using these metrics. However, the code summarization task is a difficult one – due in large part to the sizeable semantic gap between the modalities of source code and natural language. As such, while these metrics provide a general illustration of model efficacy, it can be difficult to determine the specific shortcomings of neural code summarization techniques without a more extensive qualitative investigation into their errors.

Few past studies have examined the failure modes of neural code summarization models as we outline in §6. Therefore, to further explore this topic, in this paper we perform both a qualitative and quantitative empirical comparison of three neural code summarization models. Our quantitative evaluation offers a comparison of three recently proposed models (CodeBERT (Feng et al., 2020), NeuralCodeSum (Ahmad et al., 2020), and code2seq (Alon et al., 2019)) on the Funcom dataset (LeClair and McMillan, 2019) using the smoothed BLEU-4 (Lin and Och, 2004), METEOR (Lavie and Agarwal, 2007), and ROUGE-L (Lin, 2004) metrics whereas our qualitative evaluation consists of a rigorous manual categorization of model errors (compared to ground truth captions) based on a procedure adapted from the practice of open coding (Miles et al., 2013). In summary, this paper makes the following contributions:

- We offer a quantitative comparative analysis of the CodeBERT, NeuralCodeSum, and code2seq models applied to the task of Java method summarization in the Funcom dataset. The results of this analysis illustrate that the CodeBERT model performs best to a statistically significant degree, achieving a BLEU-4 score of 24.15, a METEOR score of 30.34, and a ROUGE-L score of 35.65.
- We conduct a qualitative investigation into the various prediction errors made by our three studied models and derive a taxonomy of error modes across the various models. We also offer a discussion about differences in errors made across models and suggestions for model improvements.
- We offer resources on GitHub[2] and Zenodo[3] for replicating our experiments, including code and trained models, in addition to all of the data and examples used in our qualitative analysis of model errors.

2 Background: Deep Learning for Code Summarization

This section outlines necessary background regarding our chosen evaluation dataset as well as the three neural code summarization models upon which we focus our empirical investigation.

2.1 Dataset: Funcom

In this study we make use of the Funcom dataset (LeClair and McMillan, 2019).[4] We selected this dataset primarily for three reasons: (i) this dataset was specifically curated for the task of code summarization, excluding methods more than 100 words and comments with >13 and <3 words or which were auto-generated, (ii) it is currently one of the largest datasets specifically tailored for code summarization, containing over 2.1M Java methods with paired JavaDoc comments, (iii) it targets Java, one of the most popular programming languages.[5] In order to make for a feasible training procedure for our various model configurations, and to keep the dataset size in line with past work to which our studied models were applied (e.g., the size of the CodeXGlue dataset from Lu et al. (2021), containing approximately 180000 Java methods and JavaDoc pairs, to which CodeBERT was applied) we chose to use the first 500,000 method-comment pairs from the *filtered* Funcom dataset for our experiments. Note that we did not use the *tokenized* version of the dataset as provided by LeClair and McMillan (2019) as each of our models has unique pre-processing constraints, described in detail in Appendix B.

[2]https://github.com/SageSELab/CodeSumStudy

[3]https://doi.org/10.5281/zenodo.4904024

[4]http://leclair.tech/data/funcom/

[5]https://octoverse.github.com

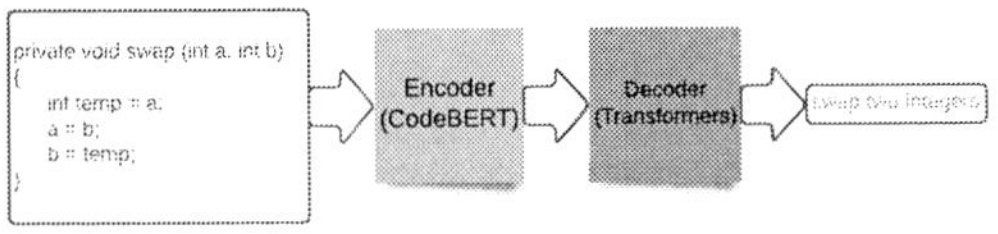

Figure 1: Code to text translation using CodeBERT.

2.2 Models

CodeBERT CodeBERT (Feng et al., 2020) is a bimodal pre-trained model used in natural language (NL) and programming language (PL) tasks. This model supports six programming language tasks in various downstream NL-PL applications, e.g., code search, code summarization, etc. The architecture of the model is based on BERT (Devlin et al., 2019), specifically following the RoBERTa-base (Liu et al., 2019) in using 125 million model parameters. The objectives of training CodeBERT are masked language modeling (MLM) and replaced token detection (RTD). Recently, Microsoft Research Asia introduced the CodeXGLUE benchmark that consists of 14 datasets for ten diversified code intelligence tasks (Lu et al., 2021). They fine-tuned CodeBERT in code-to-natural-language generation tasks. CodeBERT was used as the encoder, with a six-layer self-attentive (Vaswani et al., 2017) decoder. An architecture for code-to-text translation using the CodeBERT encoder is shown in Figure 1. The dataset Lu et al. (2021) used is derived from CodeSearchNet (Husain et al., 2019).

NeuralCodeSum The second technique we study is NeuralCodeSum (Ahmad et al., 2020). Here, the authors explored a transformer-based approach to perform the task of code summarization, using a self-attention mechanism to capture the long-term dependencies that are common in source code. In order to enable the model to both copy from already seen source code and to generate new words from its vocabulary, they employed a copy mechanism (See et al., 2017). One important distinction of source code that this model takes into account is that the absolute token position does not necessarily assist in the process of learning effective source code representations (i.e., `int a=b+c` and `int a=c+b;` both convey the same meaning). To mitigate this problem, they used the relative positioning of tokens to encode pairwise token relations. Additionally, the authors of this model also explored the integration of an abstract syntax tree (AST)-based source code representation. However, they found that the AST information did not result in a marked improvement in model accuracy.

code2seq The third model we consider in our study is code2seq (Alon et al., 2019), which is a widely utilized technique that was originally designed for the task of method name prediction. The authors of this work focused on capturing the true syntactic construction of source code by encoding AST paths. They showed that code snippets which exhibited differences in lines but that were designed for similar functionality often have similar patterns in their AST trees. To take advantage of this observation, code2seq uses an encoder-decoder architecture that attends to the constructed AST encoding to generate the resultant sequence. The authors experimented with Java method name generation as well as code captioning tasks. They compared their code captioning approach to CodeNN (Iyer et al., 2016) using BLEU score, against which it illustrated improved performance.

3 Design of the Empirical Evaluation

To evaluate the performance of our three models applied to the task of code summarization, we perform both a *quantitative* and *qualitative* evaluation centered upon the following research questions:

RQ_1: *How effective is each model in terms of predicting natural language summaries from Java methods?*

RQ_2: *What types of errors do our studied models make when compared to ground truth captions?*

RQ_3: *What differences (if any) are there between the errors made by different models?*

3.1 Evaluation Methodology for RQ_1

In this subsection, we discuss how we split the dataset, the evaluation metrics we use, and how we configure our studied models for training.

3.1.1 Dataset Preparation and Metrics

To adapt the Funcom dataset for our study, we first sampled the first 500k function-comment pairs from the *filtered* Funcom dataset into training (80%), validation (10%) and testing (10%) for our experiment, ensuring that the method-comment pairs between our training and testing datasets came from separate software projects (i.e., split by project), as suggested by the Funcom authors, in order to avoid artificial inflation of performance due to data snooping (LeClair and McMillan, 2019).

	Training	Dev	Testing
CodeXGlue	164923	5183	10955
Funcom	**400000**	**50000**	**49997**

Table 1: Data Statistics. We use the Funcom dataset.

As a comparison to past work, we illustrate the training, validation and test dataset sizes between the CodeXGLUE and Funcom datasets in Table 1. As mentioned earlier we preprocess the sampled dataset based on the requirements for each of our chosen models, and provide details in Appendix B.

Prior work has explored the use of several reference-based metrics, e.g., BLEU, METEOR, and ROUGE-L for evaluating the performance of code summarization. In our study we make use of smoothed BLEU-4 as it was previously used to evaluate the CodeBERT model (Feng et al., 2020). BLEU is the geometric average of n-gram precisions between the predicted and reference captions multiplied by a brevity penalty that penalizes the generation of short descriptions. We use the BLEU metric applying a smoothing technique (Lin and Och, 2004), which adds one count in the case of n-gram hits to address hypotheses shorter than n. In addition, we include METEOR (Lavie and Agarwal, 2007) and ROUGE-L (Lin, 2004) in our study. METEOR computes the harmonic mean between precision and recall based on unigram matches between the prediction from a model and reference, also going beyond exact matches to include stemming, synonyms, and lemmatization. ROUGE-L computes the longest common subsequence-based F-measure between the hypotheses and references.

3.1.2 Model Configurations and Training

We train, validate and test the three models described in §2 for the task of summarizing Java methods in natural language. A subset of model hyperparameters for all three studied deep learning models is shown in Table 2. We preprocess the dataset for each of the models according to their individual requirements and select the hyperparameters for each of the models based on the optimal settings from prior work. Additionally, we apply some global preprocessing that is common to all models, taken from recent work on language modeling for code (Mastropaolo et al., 2021). Initially, we remove all the comments that exist inside methods, as the commented code could lead to poor predictions. Next, all the JavaDoc comments are filtered keeping only the description of the method. Finally, we clean HTML and remove special characters from the JavaDoc captions. We provide a detailed account of our preprocessing and training techniques in Appendix B and in our publicly available resources.

Hyper-parameters	CodeBERT	Neural-CodeSum	code2seq
Batch Size	16	64	512
Beam Size	16	4	0
Optimizer	Adam	Adam	Momentum
Learning Rate	0.00005	0.0001	0.01+decay
#epochs	15	38	39

Table 2: Model Hyperparameters.

CodeBERT Model Configurations and Training: We use the open-source implementation[6] made available by Microsoft to fine-tune CodeBERT using the Funcom dataset. We utilized the optimal model configurations for this model used to train on the CodeXGlue (Lu et al., 2021) dataset with hyperparamters tuned on the Funcom dataset.

NeuralCodeSum Model Configurations and Training: We use the open-source implementation of NeuralCodeSum[7] to train the model in our study. We performed one additional preprocessing step than typical with this model, splitting camel-case words. The dropout rate is set to 0.2 and we train for a maximum of 1000 epochs. Additionally, we stop training if validation does not improve after 20 iterations.

code2seq Model Configurations and Training: We make use of the publicly available implementation of code2seq.[8] To use the Funcom dataset, we had to prepare the AST node representation using a modified dataset build script.[9] The original dataset build script was designed to predict the method name whereas we modify it to predict summaries. One problem we faced representing Funcom methods as ASTs is that there were some code examples which could not be parsed into an AST representation mainly because of the imposed minimum code length threshold and the method not having

[6] https://github.com/microsoft/CodeXGLUE/tree/main/Code-Text/code-to-text

[7] https://github.com/wasiahmad/NeuralCodeSum

[8] https://github.com/tech-srl/code2seq

[9] https://github.com/LRNavin/AutoComments

any AST-Paths. As a result, we were able to train code2seq on only a subset of the Funcom dataset ($40009/50000 \approx 80.02\%$). To train the model we made use of large batch sizes (e.g., 256 and 512) as we noted smaller batch sizes resulted in instability. As code2seq was originally designed to predict method names, we also made some changes in the model parameters to facilitate longer prediction sequences, which we give in Appendix A.

3.2 Evaluation Methodology for RQ_2 & RQ_3

We performed a manual, qualitative analysis on the output of the three models[10] to answer $\mathbf{RQ_2}$ and $\mathbf{RQ_3}$ in order to better understand and compare the various types of errors each model makes. The methodology we follow to categorize the model prediction errors follows a procedure inspired by open coding (Miles et al., 2013), which has been used in prior studies to categorize large numbers of software project artifacts (Linares-Vásquez et al., 2017, *inter alia*). Initially, we randomly selected a small number of samples from our validation split of the Funcom dataset, and applied each of our three models to generate captions. The four annotators[11] then met and discussed the samples to derive an initial set of labels that described deviations from the ground truth. We found that 15 methods (each with three predictions, one from each of our studied models) were enough to reach an initial agreement on the labels. Note that we use the ground truth captions as a "gold set" in order to orient our analysis to a shared understanding among annotators and to limit potential subjectivity.

Next, we conducted two rounds of *independent* labeling, wherein three annotators independently coded a samples of method-comment pairs and predicted comments, such that two annotators independently coded each sample. Here we define a "sample" as a method $\leftrightarrow$ gold-comment pair, *and* the three resulting predictions from CodeBERT, NeuralCodeSum, and code2seq respectively for the method. During this process, annotators were free to add additional labels outside of the initial set if they deemed it necessary. The first round of labeling consisted of 148 samples in total, amounting to $148 \times 3 = 444$ predictions from our studied models. After the independent labeling process, the authors met to resolve the conflicts among the labels. This initial round of coding resulted in a disagreement on $\approx 82\%$ of the samples wherein author discussion was needed in order to derive a common agreed upon label. There were two main reasons for this relatively high rate of disagreement: (i) the authors created some category labels with similar semantic meanings, but different labels, and (ii) some of the authors had different interpretations of shared meanings. However, through an extensive discussion, the conflicts were resolved and a shared understanding reached. The second round of independent labeling consisted of 50 samples, and resulted in a disagreement rate of only $\approx 27\%$, illustrating the stronger consensus among authors. We derive the taxonomy presented in §4 from labels present after both rounds of our open coding procedure.

[10]Some examples of the predictions are shown in Appendix C

[11]All annotators are also authors of this study.

4 Evaluation Results

In this section, we will discuss the *quantitative* and *qualitative* results from our empirical study in order to answer our research questions.

4.1 RQ_1 Results: Evaluation Based on Reference-Based Metrics

To perform the evaluation on the Funcom dataset, we use the optimal hyper-parameters shown in Table 2 for the three deep learning models. NeuralCodeSum could not predict natural language descriptions for some examples (≈ 80). The most likely reason for this situation is the errors in processing code or docstring tokens. Table 3 shows the quantitative results obtained based on smoothed BLEU-4, METEOR, and ROUGE-L scores. The results show that CodeBERT performs best among the three models. We believe that the reason we observe CodeBERT achieving this level of performance is that this model is pre-trained on both bimodal data and unimodal data (wherein bimodal data refers to the coupled code and natural language pairs and unimodal data refers to either natural language descriptions without code snippets or code snippets without natural language descriptions (Feng et al., 2020)).

Statistical significance In addition to calculating the evaluation scores (i.e. smoothed BLEU-4, METEOR, ROUGE), we conducted statistical significance tests for all three metrics to assess the validity of the obtained results. We took 19009 examples from the test dataset and used pairwise bootstrap re-sampling (Koehn, 2004) between all

Models	Smoothed BLEU-4	METEOR	ROUGE-L
CodeBERT	**24.15**	**30.34**	**35.65**
NeuralCodeSum	21.50	27.78	33.71
code2seq	18.61	27.31	33.52

Table 3: Evaluation Results with three metrics. CodeBERT is consistently better than the other two models.

3 model predictions. In comparison to NeuralCodeSum, we found CodeBERT performs better with a mean score increase (BLEU-4 2.8, METEOR 2.9, ROUGE 2.2) at a 95% confidence interval, thus indicating a performance delta that is statistically significant.

4.2 RQ_2 Results: Types of errors

In the first round of our study that included $148 \times 3 = 444$ samples, we were able to classify the errors for 398 generated natural language descriptions from the models from the validation dataset. The remaining 46 descriptions that were not classified as predictions were not made by the models due to errors in parsing and one error in processing code tokens. This singular error was due to the fact an entire code snippet was commented out, and our models do not process commented code. Thus, we did not include the predictions for the three different models for that code snippet in our study. In the other 43 cases, the code2seq model could not generate predictions because the model was not able to parse the AST.

Our error taxonomy derived after both rounds of the open coding process is shown in Figure 2. The taxonomy consists of seven high-level categories with each consisting of multiple lower-level sub-categories. To elaborate, `Semantically Unrelated to Code` is a sub-category of `Incorrect Semantic Information`. Note that one category `Consistent with Ground Truth` is dedicated to those captions that generally *matched* the ground truth, which we include for completeness. The numbers that are shown beside the name of the sub-categories illustrate the number of errors for CodeBERT, NeuralCodeSum, and code2seq respectively. The numbers shown beside the categories' names represent the cumulative sum of the sub-categories. We provide a small number of examples of these categorizations in Appendix C, and provide all labeled examples in our public resources on GitHub and Zenodo. We make the following notable observations resulting from our derived taxonomy:

- Encouragingly, among the samples studied, the largest category of samples did not display significant errors, falling into the `Consistent with Ground Truth` category ($162/535 \approx 30.28\%$). This category is the most frequent among all, but we do see CodeBERT (unsurprisingly) exhibit the largest number of reasonable summaries.
- The most prevalent error category exhibited among our studied models was that of `Missing Information` ($148/535 \approx 27.66\%$) followed by the `Incorrect Construction` category ($110/535 \approx 20.56\%$). This seems to indicate that one of the biggest struggles for current neural code summarization techniques is related to the inclusion of various types of necessary information in the summary itself, followed by issues in properly constructing comment syntax.
- The models also either incorrectly recognized or failed to recognize salient identifiers that were needed to understand method functionality in a non-negligible number of cases ($71/535 \approx 13.2\%$). This suggests that mechanisms for identifying *focal identifiers* i.e., those that might prominently contribute to describing the functionality, could be beneficial, similar to past work on identifying focal methods (Qusef et al., 2010).
- Some of the models exhibited generated summaries that over-generalized to the detriment of the summary meaning ($49/535 \approx 9.15\%$) , whereas very few summaries contained extraneous information.
- Further study is needed to gain a better understanding of the various facets of the *critical information* and *non-critical* information that captions were missing. For instance, we plan to explore whether the necessary information is contained within the code itself, or perhaps in semantically related methods. We leave this for future work.

4.3 RQ_3 Results: Comparison of three different models

One advantage of the formulation of our empirical study is that we are able to compare the various shortcomings of our studied models as they relate

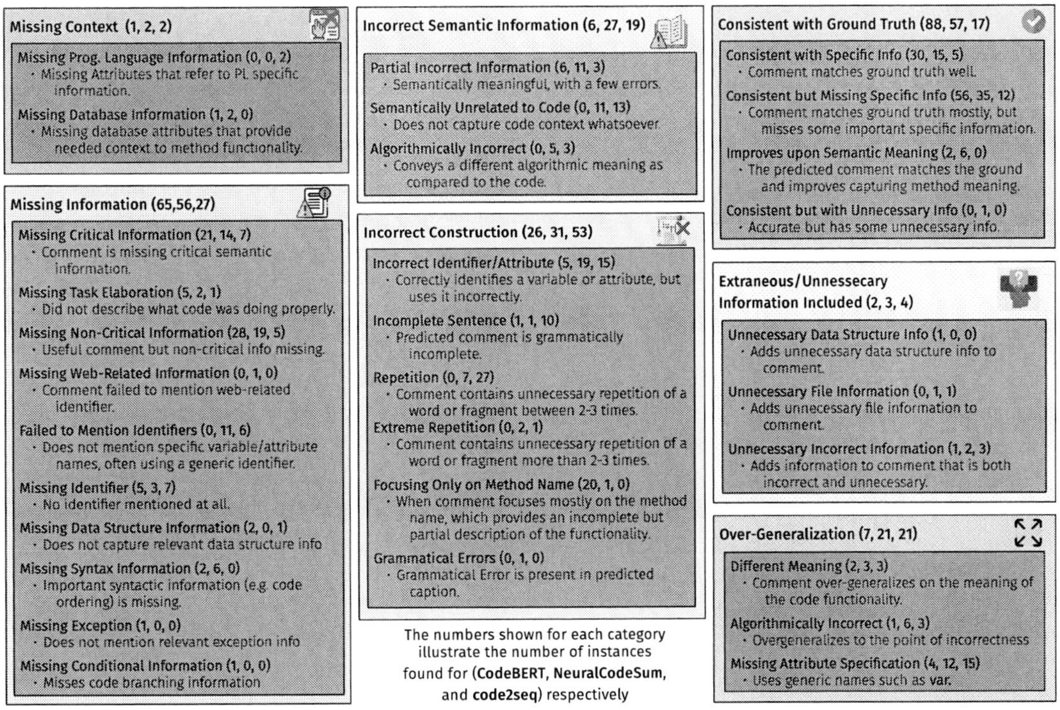

Figure 2: Taxonomy of the Errors Between the Generated Summaries and the Ground Truth

to our qualitative error analysis. To this end, we make the following notable observations:

- The most frequent error categories for CodeBERT and NeuralCodeSum are `Consistent but Missing Specific Information` (CodeBERT: $56/197 \approx 28.42\%$ and NeuralCodeSum: $35/197 \approx 17.77\%$). However, for code2seq, the most frequent category is `Repetition` ($27/141 \approx 19.15\%$).

- A non-negligible number of predictions from CodeBERT fall into the `focusing Only on the Method Name` category ($20/197 \approx 10.15\%$). This may suggest a reliance of the model on descriptive method names in order to produce reasonable summaries.

- NeuralCodeSum and code2seq produce a small number of predictions that are `Semantically Unrelated to Code`. However, we did not find any such cases for CodeBERT.

- Similar to our quantitative evaluation, we find that CodeBERT performs best, but suffers from a large number of errors related to `Missing Information`. In future work, we will investigate the adaptation of source coverage techniques (Cohn et al., 2016; Mi et al., 2016) to our task to mitigate this issue.

5 Discussion & Learned Lessons

Takeaway 1: The CodeBERT model illustrates improved performance on the Funcom dataset as compared to CodeXGLUE, likely due to the filtering steps undertaken in its construction. Previously, the CodeBERT model was fine-tuned on the CodeXGlue dataset and the smoothed BLEU-4 score obtained on the Java dataset was 17.65 (Lu et al., 2021). However, we fine-tuned the model on the Funcom dataset and obtained a smoothed BLEU-4 score of 24.15. We believe there are two primary contributing factors to this observation: 1) A higher volume of data, and 2) filtering strategies. CodeXGLUE only provides 164923 training examples, whereas we used 400000 Java Methods and Javadoc pairs during he fine-tuning process. Moreover, The CodeXGLUE dataset is obtained from CodeSearchNet and the documents that contain special tokens (e.g., <img> or https:) are filtered. In our preprocessing, we did not completely remove such data in the preprocessing; we only remove the HTML and special characters from the JavaDoc captions. We hypothesize that such characters may contain important information and

as such lead to more effective predicted summaries.
Takeaway 2: Models that rely on statically parsing source code can lead to high numbers of missing/incomplete predictions. The preprocessing for the code2seq model includes generating strings from the AST node representation of each method. Unfortunately, it is difficult (or impossible) to construct a suitable AST representation for methods that fall under a certain token length threshold. As a result, about 19.98% of the original dataset could not be fed into the code2seq testing module, and for which we could not generate any prediction for these examples.
Takeaway 3: Some of the generated summaries provide a semantic meaning similar to the ground truth, despite exhibiting fewer n-gram matches. Our studied models can generate summaries that contain relevant semantic information which can be useful for code comprehension despite not perfectly matching the ground truth. For instance, let's consider the following example ground truth for a Java method, *"this method sets the text for the heading on the component"*. The generated summary from the CodeBERT model is *"sets the heading caption"*. Comparing these two descriptions will not necessarily result in a high BLEU-4 score. This suggests that a modification to the evaluation procedure for these models may provide a more realistic characterization of model performance in practice. For instance, measuring BERTScore in addition to other metrics for evaluation (Zhang et al., 2020b)[12] may help to better capture semantic similarities compared to purely symbolic similarities.
Takeaway 4: Future techniques for Neural Code Summarization should carefully consider techniques for mitigating potential errors related to *Missing Information*, and *Incorrect Construction* as these are the most prevalent error types observed in our taxonomy. Our error taxonomy provides concrete indicators on where different types of models stand to gain performance in order to make them useful for downstream deployment. In particular, we suggest that future research focuses on rectifying `Missing Critical Information` and `Missing Non-Critical Information` rather than `Grammatical Errors` or `Unnecessary File Information`.
Takeway 5: Future studies should explore the combination of AST traversal based and self-attention mechanism-based approaches to perform robust comment generation. AST-based approach is useful to provide syntax level information and it follows the structural tree traversal method to capture the global information. At the same time, we can see this approach is prone to errors like `Repetition` and `Semantically Unrelated to Code`. On the other hand, a self-attention mechanism is useful to capture the local information. So a multi-modal approach where standard encoders can be utilized to combine both AST-based and attention-based approaches can be a viable direction to explore further.
Takeway 6: Robust evaluation metric(s) should be developed that specifically focus on source code - natural language translation. Source code is fundamentally different from the natural language from a number of perspectives. For instance, it exhibits less significant word order dependency, the significance of appropriate syntax naming and mentioning, etc. So a robust code to natural language translation evaluation metric should consider assessment from both local and global levels. Standard machine translation metrics like BLEU, METEOR, ROUGE do not fully cover these factors. As such, we encourage future work to study and develop new forms of automated metrics for assessing this special case of machine translation.

6 Related Work

6.1 Code to Comment Translation

Source code summarization is a topic of great interest in software engineering research. The aim is to automate a portion of the software documentation process by automatically generating summaries of a given granularity for a source code snippet (e.g., methods) to save developer effort. Techniques have evolved from using more traditional Information Retrieval (IR) and machine learning methods to utilizing artificial neural networks.

One of the earliest deep-learning-based source code summarization techniques is that by Iyer et al. (2016). The authors used an attention-based neural network to generate NL summaries from source code. The approach was applied to the C# programming language and SQL. Given the strong syntax associated with programming languages, researchers have also experimented with utilizing AST information for source code summarization. Hu et al. (2018) used an AST traversal method to

[12] `https://github.com/Tiiiger/bert_score`

generate summaries. Additionally, LeClair et al. (2019) utilized structural code information by encoding ASTs. Our goal in this study is to provide an overview on the performance of a variety of techniques, both sequence based (i.e., CodeBERT, NeuralCodeSum), and structure-based (i.e., code2seq), in order to examine differences in quantitative and qualitative performance across different types of models. Recently, a more complex retrieval-augmented mechanism was introduced that combines both retrieval and generation-based methods for code to comment translation (Liu et al., 2021). Finally, Bansal et al. (2021) recently proposed a method that uses a vectorized representation of source code files. We plan to explore additional techniques such as these in future work.

6.2 Empirical Studies of Code Summaries and Code Summarization

Although many deep learning models are capable of generating summaries from source code, very few researchers have focused on evaluating the errors made by the models from a human perspective. During an early study on this topic, Ying and Robillard (2013) tried to understand whether code summaries achieved the same level of agreement from multiple human perspectives. McBurney and McMillan (2016) performed a comparison based on the similarities of the summaries generated by a newly proposed model which aimed at including *context* in code summaries. However, most recent work on code summarization models, e.g., (LeClair et al., 2020; Bansal et al., 2021) depend on machine translation metrics to measure the performance of the code summarization task. However, a recent study showed a necessity of revised metrics for code summarization (Stapleton et al., 2020).

Perhaps the most closely related study to ours is that conducted by Gros et al. (2020). In this study, the authors question the validity of the formulation of code summarization as a machine translation task. In doing so, they apply code and natural language summarization models to several recently proposed code summarization datasets and one natural language dataset. They found differences between the natural language summarization and code summarization datasets that suggests marked semantic differences between the two task settings. Additionally, the authors carried out experiments which illustrate that reference-based metrics such as BLEU score may not be well suited for measuring the efficacy of code summarization tasks. Finally, the authors illustrate that IR techniques perform reasonably well at code summarization. While this study derives certain conclusions that are similar to those in our work (e.g., the need for better automated metrics) our study is differentiated by our manually derived fault taxonomy.

To the best of our knowledge, no other study has taken on a large-scale qualitative empirical study with the objective of categorizing and understanding errors between automatically generated and ground truth code summaries. Thus, we believe this is one of the first papers to take a step toward a grounded understanding of the errors made by neural code summarization techniques – offering empirically validated insights into how future code summarization techniques might be improved.

7 Conclusion & Future Work

In this work we perform both quantitative and qualitative evaluations of three popular neural code summarization techniques. Based on our quantitative analysis, we find that the CodeBERT model performs statistically significantly better than two other popular models (NeuralCodeSu, and code2seq) achieving a smoothed-BLEU-4 score of 24.15, a METEOR score of 30.34, and a ROUGE-L score of 35.65. Our qualitative analysis highlights some the most common errors made by our studied models and motivates follow-up work on improving specific model attributes.

In the future, we aim to expand our analysis to additional retrieval-augmented summarization techniques and to expand the scope and depth of our neural code summarization model error taxonomy.

References

Wasi Ahmad, Saikat Chakraborty, Baishakhi Ray, and Kai-Wei Chang. 2020. A transformer-based approach for source code summarization. pages 4998–5007.

Uri Alon, Shaked Brody, Omer Levy, and Eran Yahav. 2019. code2seq: Generating sequences from structured representations of code. In *7th International Conference on Learning Representations, ICLR 2019, New Orleans, LA, USA, May 6-9, 2019*. OpenReview.net.

Dzmitry Bahdanau, Kyunghyun Cho, and Yoshua Bengio. 2015. Neural machine translation by jointly learning to align and translate. *CoRR*, abs/1409.0473.

Aakash Bansal, Sakib Haque, and Collin McMillan. 2021. Project-level encoding for neural source code summarization of subroutines.

Kent Beck, Mike Beedle, Arie van Bennekum, Alistair Cockburn, Ward Cunningham, Martin Fowler, James Grenning, Jim Highsmith, Andrew Hunt, Ron Jeffries, Jon Kern, Brian Marick, Robert C. Martin, Steve Mellor, Ken Schwaber, Jeff Sutherland, and Dave Thomas. 2001. Manifesto for agile software development.

Jie-Cherng Chen and Sun-Jen Huang. 2009. An empirical analysis of the impact of software development problem factors on software maintainability. *J. Syst. Softw.*, 82(6):981–992.

Trevor Cohn, Cong Duy Vu Hoang, Ekaterina Vymolova, Kaisheng Yao, Chris Dyer, and Gholamreza Haffari. 2016. Incorporating structural alignment biases into an attentional neural translation model. In *Proceedings of the 2016 Conference of the North American Chapter of the Association for Computational Linguistics: Human Language Technologies*, pages 876–885, San Diego, California. Association for Computational Linguistics.

Jacob Devlin, Ming-Wei Chang, Kenton Lee, and Kristina Toutanova. 2019. BERT: Pre-training of deep bidirectional transformers for language understanding. In *Proceedings of the 2019 Conference of the North American Chapter of the Association for Computational Linguistics: Human Language Technologies, Volume 1 (Long and Short Papers)*, pages 4171–4186, Minneapolis, Minnesota. Association for Computational Linguistics.

B. P. Eddy, J. A. Robinson, N. A. Kraft, and J. C. Carver. 2013. Evaluating source code summarization techniques: Replication and expansion. In *2013 21st International Conference on Program Comprehension (ICPC)*, pages 13–22.

Zhangyin Feng, Daya Guo, Duyu Tang, Nan Duan, Xiaocheng Feng, Ming Gong, Linjun Shou, Bing Qin, Ting Liu, Daxin Jiang, and Ming Zhou. 2020. CodeBERT: A pre-trained model for programming and natural languages. In *Findings of the Association for Computational Linguistics: EMNLP 2020*, pages 1536–1547, Online. Association for Computational Linguistics.

Golara Garousi, Vahid Garousi-Yusifoglu, Guenther Ruhe, Junji Zhi, Mahmoud Moussavi, and Brian Smith. 2015. Usage and usefulness of technical software documentation: An industrial case study. *Information and Software Technology*, 57:664 – 682.

David Gros, Hariharan Sezhiyan, Prem Devanbu, and Zhou Yu. 2020. Code to comment "translation": Data, metrics, baselining evaluation. In *Proceedings of the 35th IEEE/ACM International Conference on Automated Software Engineering*, ASE '20, page 746–757, New York, NY, USA. Association for Computing Machinery.

Sonia Haiduc, Jairo Aponte, and Andrian Marcus. 2010. Supporting program comprehension with source code summarization. ICSE '10, New York, NY, USA. Association for Computing Machinery.

Sepp Hochreiter and Jürgen Schmidhuber. 1997. Long short-term memory. *Neural Comput.*, 9(8):1735–1780.

Xing Hu, Ge Li, Xin Xia, David Lo, and Zhi Jin. 2018. Deep code comment generation. In *Proceedings of the 26th Conference on Program Comprehension*, ICPC '18, page 200–210, New York, NY, USA. Association for Computing Machinery.

Hamel Husain, Ho-Hsiang Wu, Tiferet Gazit, Miltiadis Allamanis, and Marc Brockschmidt. 2019. Codesearchnet challenge: Evaluating the state of semantic code search. *CoRR*, abs/1909.09436.

Srinivasan Iyer, Ioannis Konstas, Alvin Cheung, and Luke Zettlemoyer. 2016. Summarizing source code using a neural attention model. In *Proceedings of the 54th Annual Meeting of the Association for Computational Linguistics (Volume 1: Long Papers)*, pages 2073–2083, Berlin, Germany. Association for Computational Linguistics.

Philipp Koehn. 2004. Statistical significance tests for machine translation evaluation. In *Proceedings of the 2004 Conference on Empirical Methods in Natural Language Processing*, pages 388–395, Barcelona, Spain. Association for Computational Linguistics.

Amy N. Langville and Carl D. Meyer. 2006. *Google's PageRank and Beyond: The Science of Search Engine Rankings*. Princeton University Press, USA.

Alon Lavie and Abhaya Agarwal. 2007. Meteor: An automatic metric for mt evaluation with high levels of correlation with human judgments. In *Proceedings of the Second Workshop on Statistical Machine Translation*, StatMT '07, page 228–231, USA. Association for Computational Linguistics.

Alexander LeClair, Sakib Haque, Lingfei Wu, and Collin McMillan. 2020. Improved code summarization via a graph neural network. In *Proceedings of the 28th International Conference on Program Comprehension*, ICPC '20, page 184–195, New York, NY, USA. Association for Computing Machinery.

Alexander LeClair, Siyuan Jiang, and Collin McMillan. 2019. A neural model for generating natural language summaries of program subroutines. In *Proceedings of the 41st International Conference on Software Engineering*, ICSE '19, page 795–806. IEEE Press.

Alexander LeClair and Collin McMillan. 2019. Recommendations for datasets for source code summarization. *CoRR*, abs/1904.02660.

Chin-Yew Lin. 2004. ROUGE: A package for automatic evaluation of summaries. In *Text Summarization Branches Out*, pages 74–81, Barcelona, Spain. Association for Computational Linguistics.

Chin-Yew Lin and Franz Josef Och. 2004. Orange: a method for evaluating automatic evaluation metrics for machine translation. In *The 20th International Conference on Computational Linguistics (COLING 2004)*, pages 501–507. COLING.

Mario Linares-Vásquez, Gabriele Bavota, Michele Tufano, Kevin Moran, Massimiliano Di Penta, Christopher Vendome, Carlos Bernal-Cárdenas, and Denys Poshyvanyk. 2017. Enabling mutation testing for android apps. In *Proceedings of the 2017 11th Joint Meeting on Foundations of Software Engineering*, ESEC/FSE 2017, page 233–244, New York, NY, USA. Association for Computing Machinery.

Shangqing Liu, Yu Chen, Xiaofei Xie, Jing Kai Siow, and Yang Liu. 2021. Retrieval-augmented generation for code summarization via hybrid {gnn}. In *International Conference on Learning Representations*.

Yinhan Liu, Myle Ott, Naman Goyal, Jingfei Du, Mandar Joshi, Danqi Chen, Omer Levy, Mike Lewis, Luke Zettlemoyer, and Veselin Stoyanov. 2019. Roberta: A robustly optimized BERT pretraining approach. *CoRR*, abs/1907.11692.

Shuai Lu, Daya Guo, Shuo Ren, Junjie Huang, Alexey Svyatkovskiy, Ambrosio Blanco, Colin Clement, Dawn Drain, Daxin Jiang, Duyu Tang, Ge Li, Lidong Zhou, Linjun Shou, Long Zhou, Michele Tufano, Ming Gong, Ming Zhou, Nan Duan, Neel Sundaresan, Shao Kun Deng, Shengyu Fu, and Shujie Liu. 2021. Codexglue: A machine learning benchmark dataset for code understanding and generation.

Antonio Mastropaolo, Simone Scalabrino, Nathan Cooper, David Nader Palacio, Denys Poshyvanyk, Rocco Oliveto, and Gabriele Bavota. 2021. Studying the usage of text-to-text transfer transformer to support code-related tasks.

P. W. McBurney and C. McMillan. 2016. Automatic source code summarization of context for java methods. *IEEE Transactions on Software Engineering*, 42(2):103–119.

Paul W. McBurney and Collin McMillan. 2014. Automatic documentation generation via source code summarization of method context. In *Proceedings of the 22nd International Conference on Program Comprehension*, ICPC 2014, page 279–290, New York, NY, USA. Association for Computing Machinery.

Haitao Mi, Baskaran Sankaran, Zhiguo Wang, and Abe Ittycheriah. 2016. Coverage embedding models for neural machine translation. In *Proceedings of the 2016 Conference on Empirical Methods in Natural Language Processing*, pages 955–960, Austin, Texas. Association for Computational Linguistics.

Matthew B. Miles, A. Michael Huberman, and Johnny Saldaña. 2013. *Qualitative data analysis: a methods sourcebook*. Thousand Oaks, Califorinia: SAGE Publications, Inc., [2014] ©2014.

Kishore Papineni, Salim Roukos, Todd Ward, and Wei-Jing Zhu. 2002. Bleu: A method for automatic evaluation of machine translation. ACL '02, page 311–318, USA. Association for Computational Linguistics.

Abdallah Qusef, Rocco Oliveto, and Andrea De Lucia. 2010. Recovering traceability links between unit tests and classes under test: An improved method. In *2010 IEEE International Conference on Software Maintenance*, pages 1–10.

Abigail See, Peter J. Liu, and Christopher D. Manning. 2017. Get to the point: Summarization with pointer-generator networks. *Proceedings of the 55th Annual Meeting of the Association for Computational Linguistics (Volume 1: Long Papers)*.

Sean Stapleton, Yashmeet Gambhir, Alexander LeClair, Zachary Eberhart, Westley Weimer, Kevin Leach, and Yu Huang. 2020. A human study of comprehension and code summarization. In *Proceedings of the 28th International Conference on Program Comprehension*, ICPC '20, page 2–13, New York, NY, USA. Association for Computing Machinery.

Ashish Vaswani, Noam Shazeer, Niki Parmar, Jakob Uszkoreit, Llion Jones, Aidan N. Gomez, undefinedukasz Kaiser, and Illia Polosukhin. 2017. Attention is all you need. NIPS'17, page 6000–6010, Red Hook, NY, USA. Curran Associates Inc.

Yao Wan, Zhou Zhao, Min Yang, Guandong Xu, Haochao Ying, Jian Wu, and Philip S. Yu. 2018. Improving automatic source code summarization via deep reinforcement learning. In *Proceedings of the 33rd ACM/IEEE International Conference on Automated Software Engineering*, ASE 2018, page 397–407, New York, NY, USA. Association for Computing Machinery.

Annie T. T. Ying and Martin P. Robillard. 2013. Code fragment summarization. ESEC/FSE 2013, page 655–658, New York, NY, USA. Association for Computing Machinery.

Jian Zhang, Xu Wang, Hongyu Zhang, Hailong Sun, and Xudong Liu. 2020a. Retrieval-based neural source code summarization. In *Proceedings of the ACM/IEEE 42nd International Conference on Software Engineering*, ICSE '20, page 1385–1397, New York, NY, USA. Association for Computing Machinery.

Tianyi Zhang, Varsha Kishore, Felix Wu, Kilian Q. Weinberger, and Yoav Artzi. 2020b. Bertscore: Evaluating text generation with bert.

Junji Zhi, Vahid Garousi-Yusiflu, Bo Sun, Golara Garousi, Shawn Shahnewaz, and Guenther Ruhe. 2015. Cost, benefits and quality of software development documentation. *J. Sys. Sof.*

Yuxiang Zhu and Minxue Pan. 2019. Automatic code summarization: A systematic literature review. *CoRR*, abs/1909.04352.

A Hyper-parameters

In Table 4, we show the hyper-parameters that are used in our adapted models. Code2seq model could not be trained using batch size 64 or 128 because of the instability occurred from the longer comment length. Originally, this model was designed to predict the method name. So we trained the model using batch size 512 in our final experiment and it required 39 epochs to train the model.

Hyper-parameters	**CodeBERT**	**Neural-CodeSum**	**Code2Seq**
Maximum Source Length	256	150	200
Batch Size	16	64	512
Beam Size	16	4	0
Optimizer	Adam	Adam	Momentum
Learning Rate	0.00005	0.0001	0.01+exp. decay
#epochs	15	38	39
Dropout rate	0.1	0.2	0.25
#Attention heads	12	8	–
Early stopping	True	True	True
#layers	6	6	–

Table 4: Model Hyperparameters

B Data Prepossessing

We had to perform several preprocessing steps to make the dataset ready for training. Among all the three models, we removed comments inside methods, removed tags, clean HTML, lowercasing characters, removing special characters. For the NeuralCodeSum model, we applied an additional sub-tokenization step. For code2seq, we needed to prepare the AST representation of the code snippets. To do this, we used a modified `JavaExtractor`[13] which locates the Java methods and put them in a file where each line is for one method. Subtokenization is performed in between to tokenize the CamelCase attributes (i.e. `["ArrayList"->["Array", "List"]]`). The original dataset build script was designed to put the method name in the prediction window. The modified one puts the comment instead of a method name. In Table 5, a Java code, comment and the equivalent one line dataset instance (AST representation) is presented. While performing this step, some methods could not be parsed as this AST representation mainly because of the minimum method length threshold required for the parsing. In total, we could transform 80.02% of our training dataset on which we trained the code2seq model. All the steps used in preprocessing are shown in Table 6.

C Case Study

In Table 7, model predictions are given with the ground truth and assigned error categories.

[13]`https://github.com/LRNavin/AutoComments`

Original Method	`public Type getType() { return m_type; }`
Comment	returns the type of this technical information
AST represtation	`returns|the|type|of|this|technical|information type,Cls0|Mth|Nm1,get|type type,Cls0|Mth|Bk|Ret|Nm0,m|type get|type,Nm1|Mth|Bk|Ret|Nm0,m|type`

Table 5: AST representation of java method for code2seq training

Preprocessing	**CodeBERT**	**Neural-CodeSum**	**Code2Seq**
removed comments inside methods	✓	✓	✓
removed tags for comments and methods	✓	✓	✓
HTML cleaning	✓	✓	✓
Sub-tokenization		✓	✓
Lowercase	✓	✓	✓
removing special characters	✓	✓	✓

Table 6: Preprocessing

Java Method	Human written comment	Prediction (Catagory) CodeBert	NeuralCodeSum	Code2Seq
`public float getDashPhase() { return dashPhase;}`	gets the dash phase of the basicstroke	gets the dashphase (Consistent but Missing Specific Info)	returns the phase of dealpoint (Partial Incorrect Information)	get the current velocity of the current value (Semantically Unrelated to Code)
`public void setReadTimeout(int timeout) { if (0 > timeout) { this.readTimeout = timeout; }`	sets the timeout value in milliseconds for reading from the input stream	sets the read timeout (Focusing Only on Mehod Name)	sets the number of milliseconds to wait for a response before timing out (Consistent with Specific Info)	sets the timeout to read from the server (Consistent but Missing Specific Info)
`public String numRulesTipText() { return "Number of rules to find."; }`	returns the tip text for this property	gets the numrulestiptext attribute of the appletlocale object (Unnecessary Incorrect Information)	returns the number of labels in the rule set (Semantically Unrelated to Code)	returns the text of the text of the current text (Repetition)
`public Items withTotalResults(BigInteger value) { setTotalResults(value); return this;}`	sets the value of the totalresults property	sets the total results (Consistent with Specific Info)	sets the total number of items in the group (Incorrect Identifier/Attribute)	returns the total results for the given var (Missing Critical Information)
`public String getSchema() { return fSchema; }`	returns a path to the xml schema of a extension point	returns the schema (Consistent but Missing Specific Info)	returns the name of the xml schema (Missing Non-Critical Information)	returns the schema schema (Repetition)
`public boolean isCreateIds() { return createIds; }`	returns true if the model automatically creates ids and resolves id collisions	returns the createids (Partial Incorrect Information)	returns the } (Missing Syntax Information)	returns whether the is the default id (Missing Attribute Specification)
`public PromotionEligibilityRequirement withQuantity(Integer value) {setQuantity(value); return this; }`	sets the value of the quantity property	returns a quantity (Different Meaning)	sets the value of this property any previous animations are stopped (Unnecessary Incorrect Information)	sets the var (Missing Attribute Specification)
`public void setHeight(int height) { _containerHeight = height; }`	this method sets the minimum height of the table in pixels	sets the height of the container (Consistent but Missing Specific Info)	sets the height of the image (Incorrect Identifier/Attribute)	sets the height of the image (Incorrect Identifier/Attribute)
`public void testForConnection() throws Exception { serverControl.ping(); }`	try to test for a connection throws exception if unable to get a connection	test for a connection (Consistent but Missing Specific Info)	tests the connection to the server (Consistent but Missing Specific Info)	test for the getter of the property (Missing Attribute Specification)
`public void setPath(Path path) { mPath = path.toString(); }`	sets the value of the "path" attribute	sets the path (Consistent but Missing Specific Info)	sets the path (Consistent but Missing Specific Info)	sets the path to the path of the path are not relative to the path of the path (Extreme Repetition)

Table 7: Detailed case study of model predictions with ground truth

ConTest: A Unit Test Completion Benchmark featuring Context

Johannes Villmow, Jonas Depoix, Adrian Ulges
RheinMain University of Applied Sciences
Wiesbaden, Germany
{johannes.villmow, adrian.ulges}@hs-rm.de
jonas.depoix@web.de

Abstract

We introduce ConTest, a benchmark for NLP-based unit test completion, the task of predicting a test's assert statements given its setup and focal method, i.e. the method to be tested. ConTest is large-scale (with $365k$ datapoints). Besides the test code and tested code, it also features *context code* called by either. We found context to be crucial for accurately predicting assertions. We also introduce baselines based on transformer encoder-decoders, and study the effects of including syntactic information and context. Overall, our models achieve a BLEU score of 38.2, while only generating unparsable code in 1.92% of cases.

1 Introduction

Testing is commonly considered an important part of software development, but it tends to be neglected in practice, as developers find it rather time-consuming and tedious. This has motivated *automated* testing: Approaches such as EvoSuite (Campos et al., 2019) and Randoop (Pacheco and Ernst, 2007) can bootstrap tests with decent code coverage using static code analysis and evolutionary search. However, recent studies (Almasi et al., 2017; Shamshiri, 2015) have found the readability of those generated tests to be subpar, and have – more importantly – found that the above approaches struggle with producing "meaningful" checks that truly assert the code to behave as expected.

Therefore, recent approaches have tackled *AI-based test completion* as a research challenge for NLP-based programming, using encoder-decoder models with bidirectional recurrent networks (Watson et al., 2020) or pre-trained transformers (Tufano et al., 2020b). These models take the test's setup code, together with the targeted method call (focal method) as input and predict the test's assertion. Since this assertion is arguably the test's part which requires the most understanding of the target method, it is also the part where heuristic approaches struggle the most. Here, an AI-based approach can fill this gap and provide the most valuable addition to existing solutions.

We extend this line of research by introducing ConTest, a new contextual benchmark for automated test completion. ConTest is based on Github data. Each of its datapoints features a test method, linked with the tested focal method using a fuzzy name matching. Additionally, the test is split into segments using heuristics and static code analysis: We provide the focal method, test setup code executed before the assertions, context methods called within the setup code, and context methods called within the focal method. A manual inspection of samples estimates its ground truth's accuracy of matching the correct focal method at 94%, but we even found the falsely matched methods to be relevant to the test. Summarizing, ConTest offers the following benefits[1]:

- **Context**: ConTest includes not only the test code and focal method, but also *context code* called by either of them, including the test setup and recursively called methods from the test file or tested file. Arguably, this context is crucial for fully comprehending a test. Correspondingly, we found it to strongly improve accuracy.

- **Scale**: With $365k$ high-quality datapoints for test completion, ConTest is, to the best of our knowledge, the largest test completion dataset to date.

- **Rigorous evaluation**: When building Con-

[1]The dataset is available at https://github.com/lavis-nlp/ConTest

Proceedings of the 1st Workshop on Natural Language Processing for Programming (NLP4Prog 2021), pages 17–25
August 1–6, 2021. ©2021 Association for Computational Linguistics

TEST, we have carefully avoided bias towards simple cases. Besides common metrics such as BLEU and ROUGE, CONTEST also estimates a code's unparsable rate in an accompanied evaluation package. Finally, we also provide a *project-based split*, which enforces test completion models to generalize to projects unseen in training, a setup which we found to be particularly challenging.

- **Strong baselines**: We provide Transformer-based baseline experiments. These include (1) enriching the input source code using Abstract Syntax Trees (AST), which we found to yield improvements by 4.1 BLEU points, and (2) adding context methods called by either test code or tested code (improvements by 10.1 BLEU points). Our experiments also show that the model struggles to generalize knowledge it has gathered from tests within the same project to tests in other projects (-21 BLEU). Nonetheless, our results indicate that automated test completion is an interesting direction for future research.

2 Related Work

Our work targets the fields of automated software testing and natural language processing. Automated software testing can be divided into test generation approaches, aiming to generate the *complete* test (Tufano et al., 2020a) and test *completion* approaches, aiming to generate meaningful assert statements (Watson et al., 2020). Test completion has been tackled by rule based approaches such as Agitar (Belhumeur et al., 2004), Randoop (Pacheco and Ernst, 2007), and EvoSuite (Campos et al., 2019), which can bootstrap tests with decent code coverage using static code analysis and evolutionary search. However, recent studies (Almasi et al., 2017) have found that these approaches struggle with producing "meaningful" checks that truly assert the code to behave as expected. Furthermore these approaches require handcrafted rules in order to generate assert statements.

Recently, the focus has shifted to approach automatic software testing using natural language processing (NLP) methods. White and Krinke (2018) employ a RNN-based neural machine translation system to generate complete tests, while more recent work (Tufano et al., 2020a) adapts pre-trained transformer models such as BART (Lewis et al., 2019). This and most recent work builds on transformers (Vaswani et al., 2017), which have become ubiquitous in natural language processing for sequence-to-sequence tasks. However, the authors report that the model often had difficulties to correctly initialize the object under test, as it was lacking the context information to do so. Our benchmark CONTEST includes such context information.

Recently, test completion has been tackled with machine translation methods by Watson et al. (2020). The authors propose an RNN-based approach to assert generation called ATLAS, along with a dataset of the same name. The ATLAS dataset consists of $158,096$ tests paired with single line assert statements and is, to the best of the authors knowledge, the only available dataset for test completion available. Note that the ATLAS dataset is less than half the size of CONTEST, does not contain any context information, does not provide a project-wise split and in contrast to CONTEST contains only single line assertions. ATLAS has been used in recent studies of Tufano et al. (2020b), where the authors pre-train the transformer-based BART model on a large set of English texts and code artifacts and subsequently fine-tune it to generate assert statements. Applying their model on our dataset is an interesting direction for future research.

3 Dataset

Java has been the most used programming language in 2020, and its unit test framework JUnit has become a widely adopted industry standard (Poirier, 2018). Driven by the vast amount of open-source projects available on GitHub that employ JUnit as a testing framework, we chose to build CONTEST by scraping JUnit projects from GitHub. By limiting the projects to only one testing framework the test structure will stay more consistent throughout the dataset. Furthermore, as JUnit requires annotating tests with `@Test`, such methods can be located easily.

3.1 Data collection

We utilize the publicly available Github BigQuery Dataset (Hoffa, 2016), containing a snapshot with more than 3TB data of 2.8 million open source GitHub repositories[2]. Using BigQuery (Fernandes and Bernardino, 2015), we filter relevant projects

[2]We found using the GitHub API to be infeasible due to its rate limited of 5,000 requests per hour.

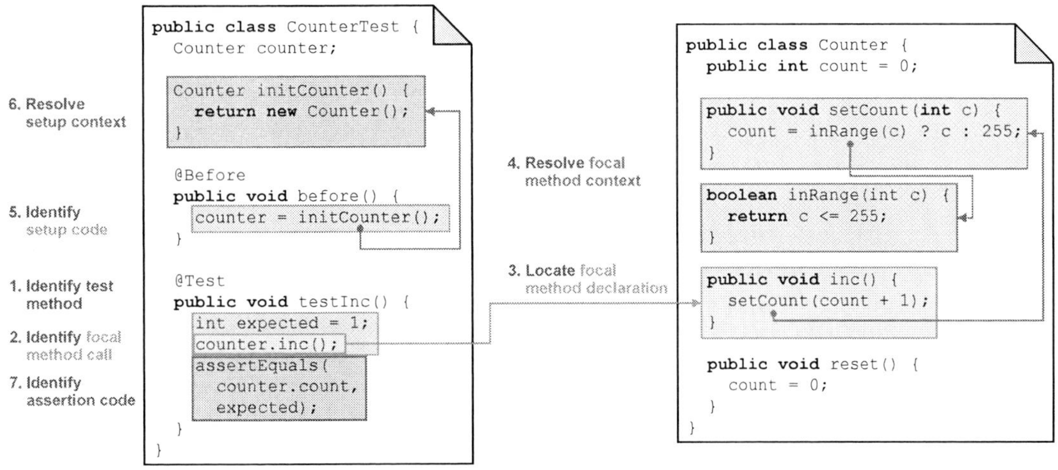

Figure 1: Components of CONTEST and steps taken to build the dataset. The task is to generate assertions (red box) given the partial test and its context. For each test we extract up to four parts: (1) the setup code of the test (green) and also include global JUnit setup code (i.e. the initialization of the `counter`), (2) code of the focal method (orange) matched using fuzzy string matching, and the source code of all additional methods that are called (recursively) in any of the two files (3) in the test setup context (purple, i.e. `initCounter`) or (4) in the focal method (blue, i.e. `setCount`, `inRange`).

by ensuring there is at least one `.java` file that contains the substring `org.junit`, an indication of an import from the JUnit package. Even though GitHub stores large amounts of code, duplicates are a major part of it (Lopes et al., 2017). We therefore exclude forks from the dataset to prevent duplicates, unless they have more than 20 GitHub stars, indicating them being different enough from the original repository to be relevant. We employ additional per sample deduplication in a later stage to further reduce duplicates. Finally, test methods are identified by matching the `@Test` annotation.

3.2 Identifying and locating focal methods

For each test method, we need to identify the test method's so-called *focal method*, i.e. the method that will be tested. Commonly, this method's name (e.g., `inc()`) is similar to the test method's name (e.g., `testInc()`). Therefore, we identify the focal method by ranking method calls within the body of the test method (referred to as *candidates*) by their token similarity to the test's method name or the test's class name[3]: We tokenize the name of the test, the name of the test class and the candidate method's names (from which we exclude JUnit assertions) by splitting them on camel and snake case into sets of tokens. We then lowercase the tokens and remove the token `test`. This way identifiers like `createAllUsers`, `create_all_users`, `CREATE_ALL_USERS`, and `test_createAllUsers` all result in the tokens `create`, `all` and `users`. We compute the following similarity based on two sets of tokens:

$$sim(T, C) := \frac{|T \cap C|}{|T|} \quad (1)$$

with T, C being sets of tokens. Let T_{name}, T_{class} be the set of tokens in the test's name/class and C_i the set of tokens in a candidate i's method name. Every unique candidate is first ranked by computing $sim(T_{name}, C_i)$ and the highest ranked candidate with a score greater than a threshold δ=0.1 chosen as the focal method. If there are multiple candidates with the same score or the score is below δ, we repeat the ranking process with T_{class}. If this process fails we consider the test as unresolvable and drop it from the dataset.

Knowing the name of the focal method, its declaration is located using JavaParser's TypeSolver feature (van Bruggen et al., 2020), which infers the type of a given AST node by analyzing surrounding nodes and the ASTs of imported modules.

In a manual evaluation on 100 randomly selected samples of our dataset we found that 94% were correctly matched and that the false positives were

[3]When matching the test name with all candidates fails, we compare the candidates with the test's class name, as sometimes tests are named by a test scenario (e.g. `testMultipleCalls` could be a test method of class `TestInc`).

also relevant to the test.

3.3 Identifying setup and assertion code

Next, we split the test method into *setup* vs. *assertion code* (green vs. red in Figure 1). Contrary to ATLAS (Watson et al., 2020), we do not only consider calls to JUnit assertion methods (like `assertEquals`) assertion code, but also the code leading up to it. This code could for example contain variable initialization or a surrounding `for`-loop, which is often essential to the assertion logic. To achieve this, all lines of code *following* the *last* focal method call (there can be multiple calls) are considered assertion code, while the preceding code lines are considered setup code.

The code line containing the last focal method call itself is considered part of the setup code (see Figure 1), unless the call happens inside a JUnit assert method (e.g., `assertEquals(counter.inc(),17))`. In this case, it is considered part of the assertion code.

In JUnit the `@Before` or `@BeforeEach` annotation (depending on the JUnit version) declares that code inside this methods should be executed before every single test in that class, or with `@BeforeClass`/`@BeforeAll` to be executed only once before all tests. Therefore, methods annotated as such are also considered part of the setup code in CONTEST.

3.4 Resolving contexts

The most notable novelty CONTEST provides is the addition of the *setup context* (purple in Figure 1) and *focal method context* (blue). We consider a method as part of such a context and thereby relevant to the task, if it is called during setup or in the focal method and belongs to any of the two java classes. Additionally, we consider methods called within the context methods as part of the context, thereby defining it recursively. We resolve those context methods using JavaParser's previously mentioned TypeSolver feature.

Since crucial parts of a focal method's logic may be outsourced to its context, we argue that adding the context of the setup code and focal method to the input of a test completion model is crucial to improve complex focal method understanding. This assumption is also backed by previous work reporting failed predictions due to missing context information (Tufano et al., 2020a).

3.5 Dataset size

Using the approach described in the previous sections 99,015 repositories were downloaded, with a total compressed size of 535GB. In these repositories 6,040,446 test methods in 1,127,415 test classes were found. Of those test methods 2,182,225 have successfully been mapped to their target method in one of 430,934 target classes. On the other hand, 3,858,221 tests could not be mapped, as no target method was found using the heuristics and resolving described in Section 3.2. Of the successfully mapped tests the setup and assertion code was identified for 1,336,360.

Another important distinction in the data is made by the location of the focal method calls. As having focal methods calls within the assertion code would require a model trained to generate assertion to also predict focal method calls, we limit CONTEST to tests were focal method calls only occur within the setup code, thereby limiting it to 845,497 datapoints[4]. After removing duplicates and datapoints with excessively large contexts, the final dataset contains 365,450 samples.

Following common practice (Watson et al., 2020; Tufano et al., 2020a; White and Krinke, 2018), we release CONTEST alongside the data split we used to randomly distribute the dataset into training (80%), validation (10%) and test (10%) data. However, when randomly distributing datapoints into splits, the training and test split are likely to contain tests from the same project, possibly even testing the same class or method. Therefore, we believe it must be carefully investigated whether models trained using these splits exploit information encountered during training, without generalizing beyond projects. To do so, CONTEST contains another project-based split alongside the regular split, where no project has tests in more than one split.

Split	Samples	
	Random	**Project-based**
Train	292, 360	290,190
Validation	36,545	38,098
Test	36,545	37,162
Total	365,450	365,450

Table 1: Sizes of the splits in CONTEST

[4]We offer to make the unfiltered version available upon request.

3.6 Evaluation Protocol

Alongside the dataset, we release an evaluation package that can be used to evaluate new models. The evaluation protocol includes tokenization of the predictions using *javalang*. We consider only parsable predictions to be valid. The parsed token sequence is then evaluated using BLEU and ROUGE, whereas we adjust the score $s \in [0, 1]$ of each metric to take unparsable predictions into account:

$$adj(s) := s \cdot (1 - r_{up}) \tag{2}$$

where $r_{up} \in [0, 1]$ is the *unparsable rate*. This scales the metric by the ratio of parsable samples. By scaling BLEU/ROUGE in this manner, a similar effect is achieved to having an unparsable prediction score of 0, i.e. scores are penalized if the model is not able to consistently generate parsable code.

4 Approach

Our approach towards test completion is illustrated in Figure 2. Similar to prior successful work on test completion and test generation (Tufano et al., 2020a), our model utilizes a transformer encoder-decoder architecture. Additionally, we utilize *context code* that is called by either test method or focus method as additional input. Also, we investigate two fundamental ways of encoding source code: (1) in form of linearized abstract syntax trees (ASTs), and (2) a tokenized version of the source code.

Our model pipeline is illustrated in Figure 2: We process two source files containing the test and the tested code by parsing relevant code parts into ASTs, which are combined to the so-called *source tree* describing the whole test. This tree is fed into an encoder-decoder transformer, which produces a assertion's linearized AST. This is compared to the target AST using a the cross entropy loss function.

4.1 Preprocessing

Our model's input consists of four different parts: (1) the setup code of the test (green in Figure 2), (2) code of the focal method which is tested (orange), and the source code of all additional methods in any of the two files that are called (3) in the test setup context (purple) and (4) in the focal method (blue). Note, that the context resolution works recursively, so that a method which is called by a context method will also be included in the context.

Parsing: To encode the syntactic structure of the code, we parse the code snippets into abstract syntax trees (AST)[5]. Every code fragment is represented by a small tree, which we subsequently combine into a larger tree structure by adding a root node. This new tree is referred to as the *source tree* in the following. Note that context methods (3 and 4) – of which multiple ones may exist – are subsumed in separate subtrees beforehand.

Vocabulary: For the ASTs' leaf nodes – which represent identifiers occurring in code, like variable names – we follow common NLP practice (Babii et al., 2019) and tokenize them into fine-grain tokens using Byte Pair Encoding (BPE)[6]. For example an identifier like `getCount` may be splitted into `_get` and `Count`. We replace each leaf node with multiple leaf nodes with the same parent for each token in resulting list.

Linearization: Finally, to use the source tree as an input to the transformer, it is linearized in a form from which it can be decoded back into java source code: We encode each non-terminal node by an opening token <[NodeType]> and a closing token <[/NodeType]>, and render its child nodes recursively in between. Non-terminal nodes without children are represented by a single self-closing token <[NodeType]><[/]>, while value nodes simply result in a token representing their value. The target assertion's AST is encoded using the exact same preprocessing steps. In JavaParser each AST node is represented as an object, for which the corresponding source code can be retrieved by calling its `toString()` method. This enables reconstructing the source code of a linearized AST sequence.

4.2 Model

We train a vanilla transformer encoder-decoder model to perform test completion. For brevity we omit details about the transformer architecture here and refer the reader to Vaswani et al. (2017).

The linearized source trees input tokens form a sequence $\mathbf{x} = (x_1, x_2, x_3, \ldots, x_n)$, which is first processed by a transformer encoder, resulting in a sequence of continuous representations $\mathbf{z}(\mathbf{x})$, or shorter $\mathbf{z} = (\mathbf{z}_1, \ldots, \mathbf{z}_n)$. From this, the auto-regressive transformer decoder generates an out-

[5]We parse ASTs using Javaparser (van Bruggen et al., 2020).

[6]More specifically we train a sentencepiece unigram model (Kudo, 2018)

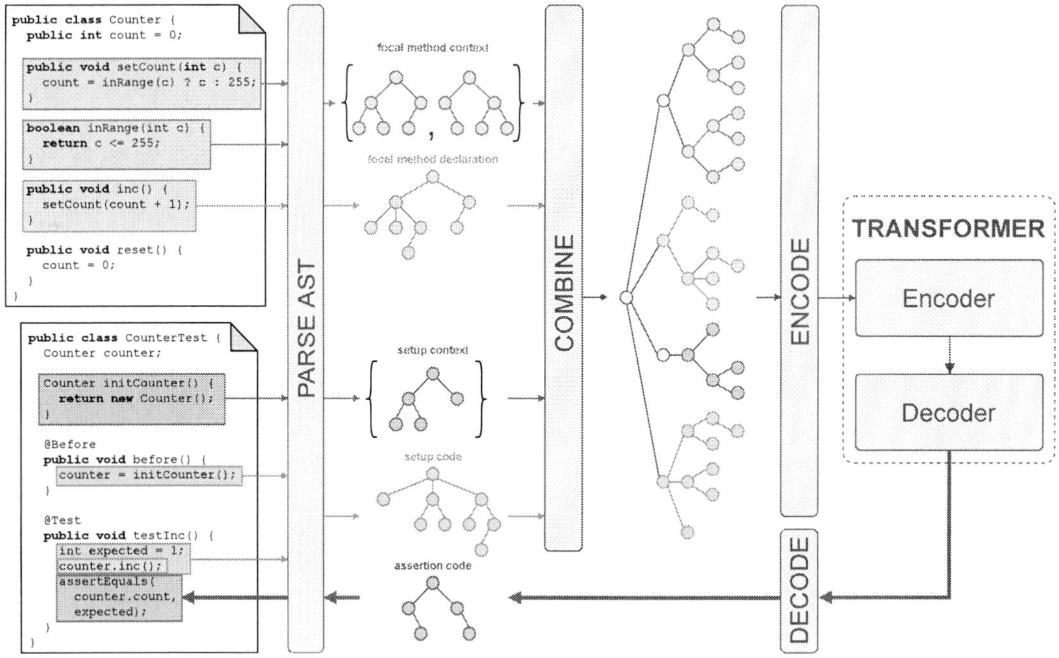

Figure 2: Visualization of our approach. We parse all four input parts into abstract syntax trees, which are then combined into one large *source tree*, that is then linearized and fed into the transformer. With this as input the transformer generates the linearized AST sequence of the target assertions (red). The generated AST is then decoded back into source code.

put token sequence $\mathbf{y} = (y_1, \ldots, y_m)$, i.e. the remainder of the test $\mathbf{x}$ (red in Figure 2). When generating token y_{i+1}, the decoder attends to the whole encoded sequence $\mathbf{z}$ as well as all previously generated symbols $y_1, \ldots, y_i$.

The sequence-to-sequence model is trained using teacher forcing (Williams and Zipser, 1989) by maximizing the conditional probability of the output sequence given the input, i.e. $p(\mathbf{y}|\mathbf{x}) = \prod_{i=1}^{m} p(y_i|y_{\leq i-1}, \mathbf{z})$ with the cross entropy loss.

5 Experiments

We evaluate our transformer-based models on CONTEST to investigate the usefulness of contextual information and compare our syntax-based AST encoding with a token-only baseline. Finally, we investigate the effect of generalizing between training and test projects using CONTEST's project-level split.

5.1 Hyperparameters and Setup

We use a standard transformer architecture consisting of 6 transformer layers in both encoder and decoder, with 8 attention heads, 2048-dimensional feed-forward layers, $d = 512$ dimensional token embeddings, and a dropout rate of 0.2. To reduce the amount of parameters, we reuse the token embeddings of the transformer encoder as input and output embedding matrices in the decoder. We train our model using the Adam optimizer (Kingma and Ba, 2014) and an inverse square root learning rate scheduler with a linear warm-up.

Relevant training hyperparameters are optimized using the Optuna framework (Akiba et al., 2019) with the Tree-structured Parzen Estimator (Bergstra et al., 2011) on the validation loss. We report results for the model with the best validation loss. For the *learning rate* we investigate the set $\{0.01, 0.005, 0.001, 0.0001, 0.00001\}$, for *warmup steps* the set $\{500, 1000, 2000, 4000\}$, and for the *batch size* the set of $\{64, 128, 256, 512\}$. For our final evaluations, we generate sequences with greedy sampling as we found this to outperform nucleus sampling (Holtzman et al., 2019) on the validation set.

We train a Byte Pair Encoding with $16k$ subwords on the training set of the dataset and use the same BPE-model throughout all experiments. We implemented our model in PyTorch using existing transformer modules and all experiments are exe-

Model	BLEU	$BLEU_1$	$BLEU_2$	$BLEU_3$	$BLEU_4$	ROUGE-1 F-Measure	ROUGE-2 F-Measure	ROUGE-L F-Measure	Unparsable Rate (%)	Max length exceeded (%)
Linearized Tree	38.19	56.31	42.35	32.85	27.15	73.00	56.43	70.64	1.92	9.06
Linearized Tree (adjusted)	37.34	55.04	41.40	32.12	26.54	70.58	55.16	69.06	1.92	9.06

Table 2: Results of our core model utilizing syntax in terms of linearized abstract syntax trees. Absolute metrics (top) are compared with their adjusted version taking non-parsable outputs into account (bottom, see Equation (2)).

	Model	BLEU	$BLEU_1$	$BLEU_2$	$BLEU_3$	$BLEU_4$	ROUGE-1 F-Measure	ROUGE-2 F-Measure	ROUGE-L F-Measure	Unparsable Rate (%)	Max length exceeded (%)
(1)	Linearized Tree (LT)	**37.05**	**55.55**	**41.22**	**31.70**	**25.98**	**70.24**	**54.39**	**68.64**	1.91	9.41
	Tokenized	32.97	49.63	36.67	28.16	23.06	68.97	53.58	67.49	**1.07**	**3.79**
(2)	Context (LT)	**37.57**	**55.73**	**41.73**	**32.25**	**26.57**	**70.61**	**55.16**	**69.05**	1.91	**9.41**
	No Context (LT)	27.49	46.86	31.80	22.31	17.18	65.14	46.94	63.51	**1.73**	16.71
(3)	Random Split (LT)	**36.46**	**54.88**	**40.58**	**31.14**	**25.47**	**69.31**	**53.46**	**67.72**	1.91	**9.41**
	Project-based Split (LT)	15.42	37.52	20.35	10.89	6.80	55.88	32.97	53.90	**1.11**	30.43

Table 3: We compare – in pairs of two – a transformer operating on a linearized tree (LT) with a variation of itself: (1) one that operates on the actual tokens and not on the tree, (2) trained without contextual information, and (3) trained and evaluated on a project-based split. Note, that the scores for (3) are not directly comparable, as the dataset differs. All scores are *adjusted.*

cuted on a server using an Intel i9-10900X CPU, 128 GB of RAM and four NVIDIA GeForce 2080 Ti GPUs with 11 GB video memory each.

5.2 Results

We present the results of our experiments in Table 2 and Table 3, where we report BLEU and ROUGE scores. For BLEU we report the cumulative BLEU4 (Papineni et al., 2002) score as the main metric, as well as the single n-gram scores ($BLUE_{1-4}$), while for ROUGE we report F-measures for ROUGE-1, ROUGE-2, and ROUGE-L scores (Lin, 2004).

In Table 2 we report the scores of our core model as described in Section 4. We evaluate once with regular scores and once with the adjusted score (compare Section 3.6) and find that the model achieves a decent BLEU. In an ablation study in Table 3 we analyze the parts of our dataset in which we compare – in pairs of two – the best performing model (transformer operating on linearized tree, denoted by "LT") with a variation of itself: (1) a "no-AST" baseline that only takes the actual tokens as input, (2) trained without contextual information, and (3) trained and evaluated on a project-based split. Note, that the scores for (3) are not directly comparable as the dataset differs. The models may fail on different evaluation samples, therefore we only report the *adjusted* metrics here (Equation (2)) and compare only datapoints for which both models were able to generate a parsable prediction. Note that this causes the scores of the best performing model to vary between experiments.

5.2.1 Syntax

We compare the transformer utilizing syntactical information by operating on a linearized tree against a regular transformer trained on tokenized and BPE'd source code. For the tokenized model we tokenize the source code using `javalang` and then apply the same BPE encoding as for the other model. In the tree, each part of the input is represented by a subtree with a unique node label. For the tokenized version we concatenate the sections of the input sequence representing test code, tested code and the respective contexts (compare Section 4.1), whereas each section is prepended by a special marker token. We found that syntax is highly beneficial when generating test assertions, as Table 3 (1) shows that the model utilizing syntax yields an improvement of 4.1 in BLEU compared to the tokenized approach. However, the tokenized approach is able to generate parsable code more often. Due to the shorter sequence length it is also able to generate longer output sequences. Recall that input and output of the AST model is longer because of the tree linearization format (compare Section 4.1).

5.2.2 Context

To evaluate the effect the context information has on the model's performance, another ablation experiment is conducted. We train a variation of the model with inputs in which context parts of the input have been removed. We drop the test setup context (Figure 1, purple) and focal method context (blue). Note that this setup is similar to other test completion datasets (i.e. ATLAS (Tufano et al., 2020a)) as those offer only parts of the test before the assertions (1) and the focal method (2) as input to the model. It is also worth noting that the model trained with context benefits from the additional information and is able to apply this knowledge to improve the quality of its predictions by 10.1 BLEU. This feels natural, as even for a developer it is often hard to understand the functionality of a method without investigating methods called within. Consider the example in Figure 1, in which there is no way of understanding the functionality of `setCount(int c)` that increments until 255 without having access to the method `inRange(int c)` called inside `setCount` which implements this check.

5.2.3 Project-level Splits

The code style within a software project mostly follows certain paradigms, and tests inside the same repository may employ the same coding style. This could be exploited by the model, which then does not need to learn the actual semantics of the code. In a last – and maybe most important – experiment we investigate how well the model is able to generalize to unseen repositories. We argue that this is the most realistic use case, as most code models will be applied to unseen repositories.

We therefore create a different version of our dataset, in which it is split by software projects and train the same model again on the resulting dataset (see Section 3.5). From Table 3 (3) we can see that the model trained on the project-based split fails to generalize across projects. This results in a BLEU score of 15.4, around half of what the model on the random split achieves. We consider this an open challenge and are looking forward to future findings indicating whether pre-trained language models on code can improve generalization. Following previous research we would like to emphasize that project-level splits should be the golden standard if one creates a dataset for machine learning on source code (Alon et al., 2019). However, as most code datasets are build upon GitHub data one should consider test leakage when evaluating large-scale pre-trained language models for code.

6 Conclusion

We have proposed a large-scale benchmark for automatic test completion coined CONTEST. In addition to pairs of test and focal methods, our benchmark uniquely contains context and setup code, offers multiline targets, and defines project-level splits. We have shown in an ablation study that context information appears to be extremely relevant to the task of test completion, and that a sequence-to-sequence transformer baseline struggles with generalizing across projects. Future research could aim to improve cross-project generalization, for example by fine-tune large scale pre-trained language models for code (Feng et al., 2020; Roziere et al., 2021) on CONTEST.

Acknowledgements

This work was funded by German Federal Ministry of Education and Research (Program FHprofUnt, Project DeepCA (13FH011PX6)).

References

Takuya Akiba, Shotaro Sano, Toshihiko Yanase, Takeru Ohta, and Masanori Koyama. 2019. Optuna: A next-generation hyperparameter optimization framework. In *Proceedings of the 25rd ACM SIGKDD International Conference on Knowledge Discovery and Data Mining*.

M Moein Almasi, Hadi Hemmati, Gordon Fraser, Andrea Arcuri, and Janis Benefelds. 2017. An industrial evaluation of unit test generation: Finding real faults in a financial application. In *2017 IEEE/ACM 39th International Conference on Software Engineering: Software Engineering in Practice Track (ICSE-SEIP)*, pages 263–272. IEEE.

Uri Alon, Meital Zilberstein, Omer Levy, and Eran Yahav. 2019. code2vec: Learning distributed representations of code. *Proceedings of the ACM on Programming Languages*, 3(POPL):40.

Hlib Babii, Andrea Janes, and Romain Robbes. 2019. Modeling vocabulary for big code machine learning. *arXiv preprint arXiv:1904.01873*.

David Belhumeur, Dale Brenneman, and Ken Pereira. 2004. Agitator for interactive exploratory testing. Accessed: 2021-04-26.

James Bergstra, Rémi Bardenet, Yoshua Bengio, and Balázs Kégl. 2011. Algorithms for hyper-parameter optimization. In *25th annual conference on neural information processing systems (NIPS 2011)*, volume 24. Neural Information Processing Systems Foundation.

Danny van Bruggen, Federico Tomassetti, and Roger Howell. 2020. Release javaparser - 3.16.1.

José Campos, Annibale Panichella, and Gordon Fraser. 2019. Evosuite at the sbst 2019 tool competition. In *2019 IEEE/ACM 12th International Workshop on Search-Based Software Testing (SBST)*, pages 29–32. IEEE.

Zhangyin Feng, Daya Guo, Duyu Tang, Nan Duan, Xiaocheng Feng, Ming Gong, Linjun Shou, Bing Qin, Ting Liu, Daxin Jiang, and Ming Zhou. 2020. CodeBERT: A pre-trained model for programming and natural languages. In *Findings of the Association for Computational Linguistics: EMNLP 2020*, pages 1536–1547, Online. Association for Computational Linguistics.

Sérgio Fernandes and Jorge Bernardino. 2015. What is bigquery? In *Proceedings of the 19th International Database Engineering & Applications Symposium*, pages 202–203.

Felipe Hoffa. 2016. Github on bigquery: Analyze all the open source code. Accessed: 2021-04-26.

Ari Holtzman, Jan Buys, Li Du, Maxwell Forbes, and Yejin Choi. 2019. The curious case of neural text degeneration. *arXiv preprint arXiv:1904.09751*.

Diederik P Kingma and Jimmy Ba. 2014. Adam: A method for stochastic optimization. *arXiv preprint arXiv:1412.6980*.

Taku Kudo. 2018. Subword regularization: Improving neural network translation models with multiple subword candidates. *arXiv preprint arXiv:1804.10959*.

Mike Lewis, Yinhan Liu, Naman Goyal, Marjan Ghazvininejad, Abdelrahman Mohamed, Omer Levy, Ves Stoyanov, and Luke Zettlemoyer. 2019. Bart: Denoising sequence-to-sequence pre-training for natural language generation, translation, and comprehension. *arXiv preprint arXiv:1910.13461*.

Chin-Yew Lin. 2004. Rouge: A package for automatic evaluation of summaries. In *Text summarization branches out*, pages 74–81.

Cristina V Lopes, Petr Maj, Pedro Martins, Vaibhav Saini, Di Yang, Jakub Zitny, Hitesh Sajnani, and Jan Vitek. 2017. Déjàvu: a map of code duplicates on github. *Proceedings of the ACM on Programming Languages*, 1(OOPSLA):1–28.

Carlos Pacheco and Michael D Ernst. 2007. Randoop: feedback-directed random testing for java. In *Companion to the 22nd ACM SIGPLAN conference on Object-oriented programming systems and applications companion*, pages 815–816.

Kishore Papineni, Salim Roukos, Todd Ward, and Wei-Jing Zhu. 2002. Bleu: a method for automatic evaluation of machine translation. In *Proceedings of the 40th annual meeting of the Association for Computational Linguistics*, pages 311–318.

Yolande Poirier. 2018. What are the most popular libraries java developers use? based on github's top projects. Accessed: 2021-04-26.

Baptiste Roziere, Marie-Anne Lachaux, Marc Szafraniec, and Guillaume Lample. 2021. Dobf: A deobfuscation pre-training objective for programming languages.

Sina Shamshiri. 2015. Automated unit test generation for evolving software. In *Proceedings of the 2015 10th Joint Meeting on Foundations of Software Engineering*, pages 1038–1041.

Michele Tufano, Dawn Drain, Alexey Svyatkovskiy, Shao Kun Deng, and Neel Sundaresan. 2020a. Unit test case generation with transformers. *arXiv preprint arXiv:2009.05617*.

Michele Tufano, Dawn Drain, Alexey Svyatkovskiy, and Neel Sundaresan. 2020b. Generating accurate assert statements for unit test cases using pretrained transformers. *CoRR*, abs/2009.05634.

Ashish Vaswani, Noam Shazeer, Niki Parmar, Jakob Uszkoreit, Llion Jones, Aidan N Gomez, Łukasz Kaiser, and Illia Polosukhin. 2017. Attention is all you need. *Advances in neural information processing systems*, 30:5998–6008.

Cody Watson, Michele Tufano, Kevin Moran, Gabriele Bavota, and Denys Poshyvanyk. 2020. On learning meaningful assert statements for unit test cases. In *Proceedings of the ACM/IEEE 42nd International Conference on Software Engineering*, ICSE '20, page 1398–1409, New York, NY, USA. Association for Computing Machinery.

Robert White and Jens Krinke. 2018. Testnmt: function-to-test neural machine translation. In *Proceedings of the 4th ACM SIGSOFT International Workshop on NLP for Software Engineering*, pages 30–33.

Ronald J Williams and David Zipser. 1989. A learning algorithm for continually running fully recurrent neural networks. *Neural computation*, 1(2):270–280.

CommitBERT: Commit Message Generation Using Pre-Trained Programming Language Model

Tae-Hwan Jung
Kyung Hee University
nlkey2022@gmail.com

Abstract

In version control using Git, the commit message is a document that summarizes source code changes in natural language. A good commit message clearly shows the source code changes, so this enhances collaboration between developers. To write a good commit message, the message should briefly summarize the source code changes, which takes a lot of time and effort. Therefore, a lot of research has been studied to automatically generate a commit message when a code modification is given. However, in most of the studies so far, there was no curated dataset for code modifications (additions and deletions) and corresponding commit messages in various programming languages. The model also had difficulty learning the contextual representation between code modification and natural language.

To solve these problems, we propose the following two methods: (1) We collect code modification and corresponding commit messages in Github for six languages (Python, PHP, Go, Java, JavaScript, and Ruby) and release a well-organized 345K pair dataset. (2) In order to resolve the large gap in contextual representation between programming language (PL) and natural language (NL), we use CodeBERT (Feng et al., 2020), a pre-trained language model (PLM) for programming code, as an initial model. Using two methods leads to successful results in the commit message generation task. Also, this is the first research attempt in fine-tuning commit generation using various programming languages and code PLM. Training code, dataset, and pretrained weights are available at https://github.com/graykode/commit-autosuggestions.

1 Introduction

Commit message is the smallest unit that summarizes source code changes in natural language. Figure 1 shows the git diff representing code modification and the corresponding commit message. A

```
        output_mode=None,
    ):
        if max_length is None:
-           max_length = tokenizer.max_len
+           max_length = tokenizer.model_max_length

        if task is not None:
            processor = glue_processors[task]()
```

Message : fix deprecated ref to tokenizer.max_len

Figure 1: The figure above shows an example of commit message and git diff in Github. In the Git process, git diff uses unified format (unidiff [2]): A line marked in red or green means a modified line, and green highlights in '+' lines are the added code, whereas red highlights in '-' lines are the deleted code.

good commit message allows developers to visualize the commit history at a glance, so many teams try to do high quality commits by creating rules for commit messages. For example, Conventional Commits [1] is one of the commit rules to use a verb of a specified type for the first word like 'Add' or 'Fix' and limit the length of the character. It is very tricky to follow all these rules and write a good quality commit message, so many developers ignore it due to lack of time and motivation. So it would be very efficient if the commit message is automatically written when a code modification is given.

Similar to text summarization, many studies have been conducted by taking code modification $X = (x_1, ..., x_n)$ as encoder input and commit message $Y = (y_1, ..., y_m)$ as decoder input based on the NMT (Neural machine translation) model. (Jiang et al., 2017; Loyola et al., 2017; van Hal et al., 2019) However, taking the code modification without distinguishing between the added and

[1] https://conventionalcommits.org
[2] https://en.wikipedia.org/wiki/Diff

Proceedings of the 1st Workshop on Natural Language Processing for Programming (NLP4Prog 2021), pages 26–33

the deleted part as model input makes it difficult to understand the context of modification in the NMT model. In addition, previous studies tend to train from scratch when training a model, but this method does not show good performance because it creates a large gap in the contextual representation between programming language (PL) and natural language (NL). To overcome the problems in previous studies and train a better commit message generation model, our approach follows two stages:

(1) Collecting and processing data with the pair of the added and deleted parts of the code $X = ((add_1, del_1), ..., (add_n, del_n))$. To take this pair dataset into the Transformer-based NMT model (Vaswani et al., 2017), we use the BERT (Devlin et al., 2018) fine-tuning method about two sentence-pair consist of added and deleted parts. This shows a better BLEU-4 score (Papineni et al., 2002) than previous works using raw git diff. Similar to CodeSearchNet (Husain et al., 2019), our data is also collected for six languages (Python, PHP, Go, Java, JavaScript, and Ruby) from Github to show good performance in various languages. We finally released 345K code modification and commit message pair data.

(2) To solve a large gap about contextual representation between programming language (PL) and natural language (NL), we use CodeBERT (Feng et al., 2020), a language model well-trained in the code domain as the initial weight. Using CodeBERT as the initial weight shows that the BLEU-4 score for commit message generation is better than when using random initialization and RoBERTa (Liu et al., 2019). Additionally, when we pre-train the Code-to-NL task to document the source code in CodeSearchNet and use the initial weight of commit generation, the contextual representation between PL and NL is further reduced.

2 Related Work

Commit message generation has been studied in various ways. Jiang and McMillan (2017) collect 2M commits from the Mauczka et al. (2015) and top 1K Java projects in Github. Among the commit messages, only those that keep the format of "Verb + Object" are filtered, grouped into verb types with similar characteristics, and then the classification model is trained with the naive Bayes classifier.

Jiang et al. (2017) use the commit data collected by Jiang and McMillan (2017) to generate the commit message using an attention-based RNN encoder-decoder NMT model. They filter again in a "verb/direct-object pattern" from 2M data and finally used the 26K commit message data. Loyola et al. (2017) uses an NMT model similar to Jiang et al. (2017), but uses git diff and commit pairs collected from 1~3 repositories of Python, Java, JavaScript, and C++ as training data. Liu et al. (2018) propose a retrieval model using Jiang et al. (2017)'s 26K commit as training data. Code modification is represented by bags of words vector, and the message with the highest cosine similarity is retrieved. Xu et al. (2019) collect only '.java' file format from Jiang and McMillan (2017) and use 509K dataset as training data for NMT. Also, to mitigate the problem of Out-of-Vocabulary (OOV) of code domain input, they use generation distribution or copying distribution similar to pointer-generator networks (See et al., 2017). van Hal et al. (2019) also argues that the Jiang and McMillan (2017) entire data is noise and proposes a pre-processing method that filters the better commit messages.

Liu et al. (2020) argue that it is challenging to represent the information required for source code input in the NMT model with a fixed-length. In order to alleviate this, it is suggested that only the added and deleted parts of the code modification be abbreviated as abstract syntax tree (AST) and applied to the Bi-LSTM model.

Nieb et al. presented a large gap between the contextual representation between the source code and the natural language when generating commit messages. Previous studies have used RNN or LSTM model, they use the transformer model, and similarly to other studies, they use Liu et al. (2018) as the training data. To reduce this gap, they try to reduce the two-loss that predict the next code line (Explicit Code Changes) and the randomly masked word in the binary file.

3 Background

3.1 Git Process

Git is a version management system that manages version history and helps collaboration efficiently. Git tracks all files in the project in the Working directory, Staging area, and Repository. The working directory shows the files in their current state. After modifying the file, developers move the files to the staging area using the `add` command to record the modified contents and write a commit message through the `commit` command. Therefore, the commit message may contain two or more file changes.

3.2 Text Summarization based on Encoder-Decoder Model

With the advent of sequence to sequence learning (Seq2Seq) (Sutskever et al., 2014), various tasks between the source and the target domain are being solved. Text summarization is one of these tasks, showing good performance through the Seq2Seq model with a more advanced encoder and decoder. The encoder and decoder models are trained by maximizing the conditional log-likelihood below based on source input $X = (x_1, ..., x_n)$ and target input $Y = (y_1, ..., y_m)$.

$$p(Y|X;\theta) = log \sum_{t=0}^{T} p(y_t|y_{<t}, X;\theta)$$

where T is the length of the target input, y_0 is the start token, y_T is the end token and θ is the parameter of the model.

In the Transformer (Vaswani et al., 2017) model, the source input is vectorized into a hidden state through self-attention as the number of encoder layers. After that, the target input also learns the generation distribution through self-attention and attention to the hidden state of the encoder. It shows better summarization results than the existing RNN-based model (Nallapati et al., 2016).

To improve performance, most machine translations use beam search. It keeps the search area by K most likely tokens at each step and searches the next step to generate better text. Generation stops when the predicted y_t is an end token or reaches the maximum target length.

3.3 CodeSearchNet

CodeSearchNet (Husain et al., 2019) is a dataset to search code function snippets in natural language. It is a paired dataset of code function snippets for six programming languages (Python, PHP, Go, Java, JavaScript and Ruby) and a docstring summarizing these functions in natural language. A total of 6M pair datasets is collected from projects with a re-distribution license. Using the CodeSearchNet corpus, retrieval of the code corresponding to the query composed of natural language can be resolved. Also, it is possible to resolve the problem of documenting the code by summarizing it in natural language (Code-to-NL).

3.4 CodeBERT

Recent NLP studies have shown state-of-the-art in various tasks through transfer learning consisting of pre-training and fine-tuning (Peters et al., 2018). In particular, BERT (Devlin et al., 2018) is a pre-trained language model by predicting masked words from randomly masked sequence input and uses only encoder based on Transformer (Vaswani et al., 2017). It shows good perfomances in various datasets and is now extending out of the natural language domain to the voice, video, and code domains.

CodeBERT is a pre-trained language model in the code domain to learn the relationship between programming language (PL) and natural language (NL). In order to learn the representation between different domains, they refer to the learning method of ELECTRA (Clark et al., 2020) which is consists of Generator-Discriminator. NL and Code Generator predict words from code tokens and comment tokens masked at a specific rate. Finally, NL-Code Discriminator is CodeBERT after trained through binary classification that predicts whether it is replaced or original.

CodeBERT shows good results for all tasks in the code domain. Specially, it shows a higher score than other pre-trained models in the code to natural language(Code-to-NL) and code retrieval task from NL using CodeSearchNet Corpus. In addition, CodeBERT uses the Byte Pair Encoding (BPE) tokenizer (Sennrich et al., 2015) used in RoBERTa, and does not generate unk tokens in code domain input.

4 Dataset

We collect a 345K code modification dataset and commit message pairs from 52K repositories of six programming languages (Python, PHP, Go, Java, JavaScript, and Ruby) on Github. When using raw git diff as model input, it is difficult to distinguish between added and deleted parts, so unlike Jiang and McMillan (2017), our dataset focuses only on the added and deleted lines in git diff. The detailed data collection and pre-processing method are shown as a pseudo-code in Algorithm 1:

To collect only the code that is a re-distributable license, we have listed the Github repository name in the CodeSearchNet dataset. After that, all the repositories are cloned through multi-threading. Detailed descriptions of functions that collect the commit hashes in a repository and the code modifi-

Algorithm 1 Code modification parser from the list of repositories.

```
procedure REPOPARSER(Repos)
  for Repo in Repos do
    commits = get_commits(Repo)
    for commit in commits do
      mods = get_modifications(commit)
      for mod in mods do
        if filtering(mod, commit) then
          break
        end if
        Save (mod.add, mod.del) to dataset.
      end for
    end for
  end for
end procedure
```

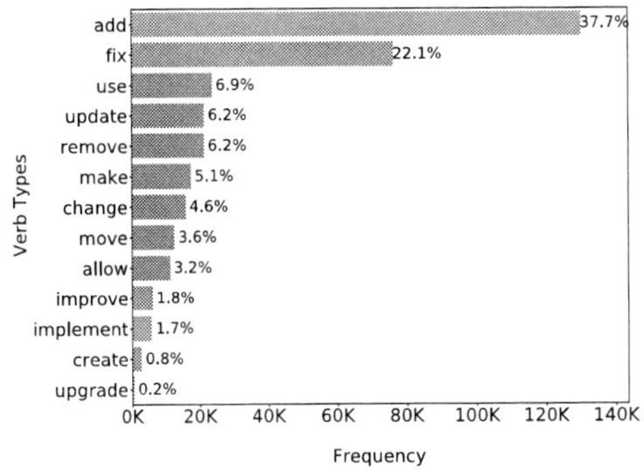

Figure 2: Commit message verb type and frequency statistics. Only 'upgrade' is not included in the high frequency, but is included in a similar way to 'update'. This refers to the verb group in Jiang and McMillan (2017).

cations in a commit hash are as follows:

- `get_commits` is a function that gets the commit history from the repository. At this time, the commits of the master branch are filtered, excluding merge commits. Commits with code modifications corresponding to 6 the program language(.py, .php, .js, .java, .go, .ruby) extensions are collected. To implement this, we use the open-source pydriller (Spadini et al., 2018).
- `get_modifications` is a function that gets the line modified in the commit. Through this function, it is possible to collect only the added or deleted parts, not all git diffs.

While collecting the pair dataset, we find that the relationship between some code modifications

	Number of Pair Dataset			Number of Repositories
	Train	Validation	Test	
Python	81517	10318	10258	12361
PHP	64458	8079	8100	16143
JavaScript	50561	6296	6252	11294
Ruby	29842	3772	3680	4581
Java	28069	3549	3552	4123
Go	21945	2699	2812	3960
Total : 345759				52462

Table 1: Dataset Statistics for each language collected from 52K repositories of six programming languages.

and the corresponding commit message is obscure and very abstract. Also, we check that some code modification or commit message is a meaningless dummy file. To filter these, we create the `filtering` function and the rules as follows.

1. To collect commit messages with various format distributions, we limit the collection of up to 50 commits in one repository.
2. We filter commits whose number of files changed is one or two per commit message.
3. Commit message with issue number is removed because detailed information is abbreviated.
4. Similar to Jiang and McMillan (2017), the non-English commit messages are removed.
5. Since some commit messages are very long, the first line is fetched.
6. If the token of code through tree-sitter[3], a parser generator tool, exceeds 32 characters, it is excluded. This removes unnecessary things like changes to binary files in code diff.
7. By referring to the Jiang and McMillan (2017) and Conventional Commits(§ 1) rules, the commit message that begins with a verb is collected. We use spaCy[4] for Pos tagging.
8. We filter commit messages with 13 verb types, which are the most frequent. Figure 2 shows the collected verb types and their ratio for the entire dataset.

As a result, we collect 345K code modification and commit message pair datasets from 52K Github repositories and split commit data into 80-10-10 train/validation/test sets. This results are shown in Table 1.

[3]https://tree-sitter.github.io/tree-sitter

[4]https://spacy.io

5 CommitBERT

We propose the idea of generating a commit message through the CodeBERT model with the our dataset (§ 4). To this end, this section describes how to feed inputs code modification ($X = ((add_1, del_1), ..., (add_n, del_n))$) and commit message ($Y = (msg1, ..., msg_n)$) to CodeBERT and how to use pre-trained weights more efficiently to reduce the gap in contextual representation between programming language (PL) and natural language (NL).

5.1 CodeBERT for Commit Message Generation

We feed the code modification to the encoder and a commit message to the decoder input by following the NMT model. Especially for code modification in the encoder, similar inputs are concatenated, and different types of inputs are separated by a sentence separator (sep). Applying this to our CommitBERT in the same way, added tokens ($Add = (add_1, ..., add_n)$) and deleted tokens ($Del = (del_1, ..., del_n)$) of similar types are connected to each other, and sentence separators are inserted between them. Therefore, the conditional-likelihood is as follows:

$$p(M|C;\theta) = log \sum_{t=0}^{T} p(m_t|m_{<t}, C; \theta),$$

$$m_{<t} = (m_0, m_1, ..., m_{t-1})$$

$$C = concat([cls], Add, [sep], Del, [sep])$$

where M is commit message tokens, C is code modification tokens and $concat$ is list concatenation function. $[cls]$ and $[sep]$ are speical tokens, which are a start token and a sentence separator token respectively. Other notions are the same as Section 3.2.

Unlike previous works, all code modifications in git diff are not used as input and only changed lines in code modification are used. Since this removes unnecessary inputs, it shows a significant performance improvement in summarizing code modifications in natural language. Figure 3 shows how the code modification is actually taken as model input.

5.2 Initialize Pretrained Weights

To reduce the gap difference between two domains(PL, NL), We use the pretrained CodeBERT as the initial weight. Furthermore, we determine that removing deleted tokens from our dataset (§ 4) is similar to the Code-to-NL task in CodeSearchNet (Section 3.3). Using this feature, we use the initial weight after training the Code-to-NL task with CodeBERT as the initial weight. This method of training shows better results than only using CodeBERT weight in commit message generation.

6 Experiment

To verify the proposal in Section 5 in the commit message generation task, we do two experiments. (1) Compare the commit message generation results of using all code modifications as inputs and using only the added or deleted lines as inputs. (2) Ablation study several initial model weights to find the weight with the smallest gap in contextual representation between PL and NL.

6.1 Experiment Setup

Our implementation uses CodeXGLUE's code-text pipeline library [5]. We use the same model architecture and experimental parameters for the two experiments below. As a model architecture, the encoder and decoder use 12 and 3 Transformer layers. We use 5e-5 as the learning rate and train on one V100 GPU with a 32 batch size. We also use 256 as the maximum source input length and 128 as the target input length, 10 training epochs, and 10 as the beam size k.

6.2 Compare Model Input Type

To experiment generating a commit message according to the input type, only 4135 data is collected from data with code modification in the '.java' files among 26K training data of Loyola et al. (2017). Then we transform these 4135 data into two types, respectively, and experiment with training data for RoBERTa and CodeBERT weights: (a) entire code modification in git diff and (b) only changed lines in code modification. Figure 3 shows these two differences in detail.

Table 3 shows the BLEU-4 values when inference with the test set after training about these two types. Both initial weights show worse results than (b), even though type (a) takes a more extended input to the model. This shows that lines other than changed lines as input data disturb training when generating the commit message.

[5]https://github.com/microsoft/CodeXGLUE

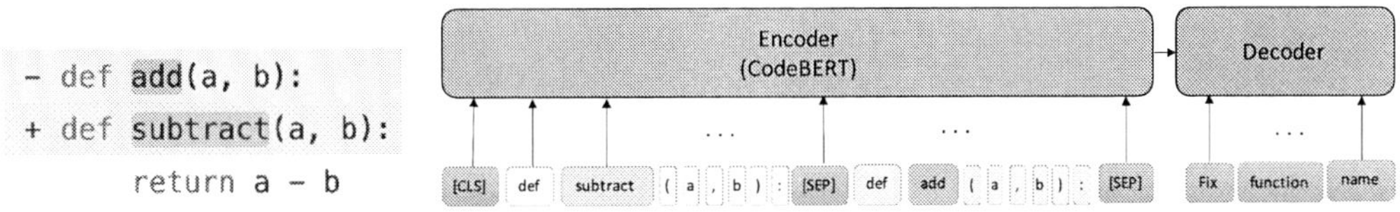

(a) Code modification in git diff (b) CommitBERT input

Figure 3: Illustration of a code modification example in git diff (a) and method of taking it to the input of CommitBERT (b). (b) shows that all code modification lines in (a) are not used, and only changed lines are as input. So, in this example, code modification (a) includes `return a - b`, but not in the model input (b).

Metric	Initial Weight	Python	PHP	JavaScript	Java	Go	Ruby
BLEU-4 (Test)	(a) Random	7.95	7.01	8.41	7.60	10.38	7.17
	(b) RoBERTa	10.94	9.71	9.50	6.40	10.21	8.95
	(c) CodeBERT	12.05	13.06	10.47	8.91	11.19	10.33
	(d) CodeBERT + Code-to-NL	**12.93**	**14.30**	**11.49**	**9.81**	**12.76**	**10.56**
PPL (Dev)	(a) Random	144.60	138.39	195.98	275.84	257.29	207.67
	(b) RoBERTa	76.02	81.97	103.48	164.32	122.70	104.68
	(c) CodeBERT	68.18	63.90	94.62	116.50	109.43	91.50
	(d) CodeBERT + Code-to-NL	**49.29**	**47.89**	**75.53**	**77.80**	**64.43**	**82.82**

Table 2: Commit message generation result for 4 initial weights. In (c), CodeBERT is used as the initial weight. And (d) uses the weight trained on the Code-to-NL task in CodeSearchNet with CodeBERT as the initial weight. As a result, it shows BLEU-4 for the test set after training and the best PPL for the validation set in the during training.

Initial Weight	Input Type	BLEU-4
RoBERTa	(a) All code modification	10.91
	(b) Only changed lines (**Ours**)	**12.52**
CodeBERT	(a) All code modification	11.77
	(b) Only changed lines (**Ours**)	**13.32**

Table 3: The result of generating the commit message for the input type after collecting 4135 data with only source code change among the data of Loyola et al. (2017). (a) uses entire git diff(unidiff) as input, and (b) uses only the changed line according to Section 5.1 as input.

6.3 Ablation study on initial weight

We do an ablation study while changing the initial weight of the model for 345K datasets in six programming languages collected in Section 4. As mentioned in 5.2, when the model weight with high comprehension in the code domain is used as the initial weight, it is assumed that the large gap in contextual representation between PL and NL would be greatly reduced. To prove this, we train the commit message generation task for four weights as initial model weights: Random, RoBERTa[6], CodeBERT[7], and the weights trained on the Code-to-NL task(Section 3.3) with CodeBERT. Except for this initial weight, all training parameters are the same.

Table 2 shows BLEU-4 for the test set and PPL for the dev set for each of the four weights after training. As a result, using weights trained on the Code-to-NL task with CodeBERT as the initial weight shows the best results for test BLEU-4 and dev PPL. It also shows good performance regardless of programming language.

7 Conclusion and Future Work

Our work presented a model summarizing code modifications to solve the difficulty of humans manually writing commit messages. To this end, this paper proposed a method of collecting data, a method of taking it to a model, and a method of improving performance. As a result, it showed a successful result in generating a commit message using our proposed methods. Consequently, our work can help developers who have difficulty writing commit messages even with the application.

Although it is possible to generate a high-quality commit message with a pre-trained model, future studies to understand the code syntax structure remain in our work. As a solution to this, CommitBERT should be converted to AST (Abstract

[6]https://huggingface.co/roberta-base
[7]https://huggingface.co/microsoft/codebert-base

Language	Reference / Generated
Python	added figsize to plot methods
	added figure size to plot_weights
PHP	added default value to fieldtype
	Added default values of the fieldtype
JavaScript	Fix missing = in delete uri
	Fixed an issue with delete
Java	Fixed the parsing of orders without a cid
	Fix bug in exchange order
Go	Use ioutil . Discard for benchmark
	Use ioutil . Discard for logging
Ruby	fixing schema validation issues with CCR export
	fixing validation of ccr export

Table 4: The result of generating the commit message for six languages (Python, PHP, Go, Java, JavaScript, and Ruby) and the corresponding reference. We used the (d) model of Table 2.

Syntax Tree) before code modification is taken into the encoder like (Liu et al., 2020).

Acknowledgments

The author would like to thank Gyuwan Kim, Dongjun Lee, Mansu Kim and the anonymous reviewers for their thoughtful paper review.

References

Kevin Clark, Minh-Thang Luong, Quoc V Le, and Christopher D Manning. 2020. Electra: Pre-training text encoders as discriminators rather than generators. *arXiv preprint arXiv:2003.10555*.

Jacob Devlin, Ming-Wei Chang, Kenton Lee, and Kristina Toutanova. 2018. Bert: Pre-training of deep bidirectional transformers for language understanding. *arXiv preprint arXiv:1810.04805*.

Zhangyin Feng, Daya Guo, Duyu Tang, Nan Duan, Xiaocheng Feng, Ming Gong, Linjun Shou, Bing Qin, Ting Liu, Daxin Jiang, et al. 2020. Codebert: A pre-trained model for programming and natural languages. *arXiv preprint arXiv:2002.08155*.

SRP van Hal, Mathieu Post, and Kasper Wendel. 2019. Generating commit messages from git diffs. *arXiv preprint arXiv:1911.11690*.

Hamel Husain, Ho-Hsiang Wu, Tiferet Gazit, Miltiadis Allamanis, and Marc Brockschmidt. 2019. Codesearchnet challenge: Evaluating the state of semantic code search. *arXiv preprint arXiv:1909.09436*.

Siyuan Jiang, Ameer Armaly, and Collin McMillan. 2017. Automatically generating commit messages from diffs using neural machine translation. In *2017 32nd IEEE/ACM International Conference on Automated Software Engineering (ASE)*, pages 135–146. IEEE.

Siyuan Jiang and Collin McMillan. 2017. Towards automatic generation of short summaries of commits. In *2017 IEEE/ACM 25th International Conference on Program Comprehension (ICPC)*, pages 320–323. IEEE.

Shangqing Liu, Cuiyun Gao, Sen Chen, Nie Lun Yiu, and Yang Liu. 2020. Atom: Commit message generation based on abstract syntax tree and hybrid ranking. *IEEE Transactions on Software Engineering*.

Yinhan Liu, Myle Ott, Naman Goyal, Jingfei Du, Mandar Joshi, Danqi Chen, Omer Levy, Mike Lewis, Luke Zettlemoyer, and Veselin Stoyanov. 2019. Roberta: A robustly optimized bert pretraining approach. *arXiv preprint arXiv:1907.11692*.

Zhongxin Liu, Xin Xia, Ahmed E Hassan, David Lo, Zhenchang Xing, and Xinyu Wang. 2018. Neural-machine-translation-based commit message generation: how far are we? In *Proceedings of the 33rd ACM/IEEE International Conference on Automated Software Engineering*, pages 373–384.

Pablo Loyola, Edison Marrese-Taylor, and Yutaka Matsuo. 2017. A neural architecture for generating natural language descriptions from source code changes. *arXiv preprint arXiv:1704.04856*.

Andreas Mauczka, Florian Brosch, Christian Schanes, and Thomas Grechenig. 2015. Dataset of developer-labeled commit messages. In *2015 IEEE/ACM 12th Working Conference on Mining Software Repositories*, pages 490–493. IEEE.

Ramesh Nallapati, Bowen Zhou, Caglar Gulcehre, Bing Xiang, et al. 2016. Abstractive text summarization using sequence-to-sequence rnns and beyond. *arXiv preprint arXiv:1602.06023*.

Lun Yiu Nieb, Cuiyun Gaoa, Zhicong Zhongc, Wai Lamb, Yang Liud, and Zenglin Xua. Coregen: Contextualized code representation learning for commit message generation.

Kishore Papineni, Salim Roukos, Todd Ward, and Wei-Jing Zhu. 2002. Bleu: a method for automatic evaluation of machine translation. In *Proceedings of the 40th annual meeting of the Association for Computational Linguistics*, pages 311–318.

Matthew E Peters, Mark Neumann, Mohit Iyyer, Matt Gardner, Christopher Clark, Kenton Lee, and Luke Zettlemoyer. 2018. Deep contextualized word representations. *arXiv preprint arXiv:1802.05365*.

Abigail See, Peter J Liu, and Christopher D Manning. 2017. Get to the point: Summarization with pointer-generator networks. *arXiv preprint arXiv:1704.04368*.

Rico Sennrich, Barry Haddow, and Alexandra Birch. 2015. Neural machine translation of rare words with subword units. *arXiv preprint arXiv:1508.07909*.

Davide Spadini, Maurício Aniche, and Alberto Bacchelli. 2018. Pydriller: Python framework for mining software repositories. In *Proceedings of the 2018 26th ACM Joint Meeting on European Software Engineering Conference and Symposium on the Foundations of Software Engineering*, pages 908–911.

Ilya Sutskever, Oriol Vinyals, and Quoc V Le. 2014. Sequence to sequence learning with neural networks. *arXiv preprint arXiv:1409.3215*.

Ashish Vaswani, Noam Shazeer, Niki Parmar, Jakob Uszkoreit, Llion Jones, Aidan N Gomez, Lukasz Kaiser, and Illia Polosukhin. 2017. Attention is all you need. *arXiv preprint arXiv:1706.03762*.

Shengbin Xu, Yuan Yao, Feng Xu, Tianxiao Gu, Hanghang Tong, and Jian Lu. 2019. Commit message generation for source code changes. In *IJCAI*.

Time-Efficient Code Completion Model for the R Programming Language

Artem Popov[1], **Dmitrii Orekhov**[13], **Denis Litvinov**[1],
Nikolay Korolev[12], **Gleb Morgachev**[14]

[1]JetBrains s.r.o., [2] Lomonosov Moscow State University,
[3] ITMO University, [4] Moscow Institute of Physics and Technology
{artem.popov, dmitrii.orekhov, denis.litvinov,
nikolai.korolev, gleb.morgachev} + @jetbrains.com

Abstract

In this paper, we present a deep learning code completion model for the R programming language. We introduce several techniques to utilize language modeling based architecture in the code completion task. With these techniques, the model requires low resources, but still achieves high quality.

We also present an evaluation dataset for the R programming language completion task. Our dataset contains multiple autocompletion usage contexts and that provides robust validation results. The dataset is publicly available.

1 Introduction

Code completion feature (for simplicity we will refer to it as autocompletion) is used in an integrated development environment (IDE) to suggest the next pieces of code during typing. Code completion engines can accelerate software development and help to reduce errors by eliminating typos.

In recent years quality improvements in the code completion task have been achieved with the transformer language models. Models with a huge amount of parameters usually demonstrate better performance (Brown et al., 2020), but in practice code completion is executed on a user laptop with limited computational resources. At the same time code completion should run as fast as possible to be considered as a convenient development tool.

In this paper, we show that the autocompletion task can be solved with a fairly good quality even with a small transformer-based model. We propose several techniques to adapt the model which was originally designed for NLP tasks to our task.

It is hard to build a good autocompletion system for dynamically typed languages without machine learning methods (Shelley, 2014). Let us consider an autocompletion of a function argument scenario. In static languages, an argument type is determined in the function definition. We can collect variables of this type from the scope in which the function is called. These variables may be used as an autocompletion output. However, in dynamic languages the argument type information is omitted. Since all dynamic languages are interpreted, variable types can not be obtained without running a program or special tools usage.

We choose a dynamic R programming language for our experiments. To the best of our knowledge, there are no papers about code completion based on deep learning for the R programming language specifically.

We also propose an evaluation dataset for the R programming language collected from the open-source GitHub projects[1]. Our dataset is divided into several groups specific for different code usage contexts. For example, there is a separate group containing package imports and another one containing function calls.

2 Related Work

There are many ways to design code completion models. One of the methods is a frequency-based system. The statistical language model is used to rank a set of possible completions extracted by the rule-based methods (Tu et al., 2014). Bruch et al. (2009) proposed proposed a ranking machine learning model, which additionally takes a feature vector describing completion context as an input.

Lately, deep learning approaches have gained popularity. Completions are generated by autoregressive models such as LSTM or transformer-based language models (Li et al., 2017) trained on a large source unlabeled code corpora. Some large models such as GPT3 (Brown et al., 2020) can even perform a full-line autocompletion with

[1]https://github.com/arti32lehtonen/rcompletion_evaluation_dataset

Proceedings of the 1st Workshop on Natural Language Processing for Programming (NLP4Prog 2021), pages 34–39
August 1–6, 2021.

promising quality. Alon et al. (2019) suggest to predict the next node of the abstract syntax tree (AST) of the program to get completions. Liu et al. (2020) propose to predict the token and its type jointly to improve completion performance for identifiers.

3 Model

3.1 Baseline model

We use conventional GPT-2 (Radford et al., 2019) architecture with Byte Pair Encoding (BPE) tokenization (Sennrich et al., 2015), but with fewer layers and heads and a lower hidden size. We train it on a standard language modeling task, predicting the next BPE token x_t from the previous ones:

$$\mathcal{L}_{lm} = \sum_t \log p(x_t | x_{<t}) \to \max \qquad (1)$$

However, we use special preprocessing to make this task easier. In particular, we apply R lexer to a source code to get so-called program tokens. We use that information to replace numerical and string literals by type-specific placeholders, delete comments and remove vector content.

At inference time we exploit beams search and softmax with temperature. To prevent generation of the repeating elements we use penalized sampling (Keskar et al., 2019).

3.2 Variable Name Substitution

As we know, transformers suffer from $O(n^2)$ complexity with n as input length. It limits their ability to exploit large contexts and therefore limits code completion quality. If we take only the last tokens as input, it can dramatically reduce a model quality in a code completion task. For example, it is very complicated to get a variable with a rare name in the model output if it is declared at the start of the program and never used after that.

While BPE tokenization allows us to represent rare words with fixed-size vocabulary, they can still have damaging effect on the training and the inference stages. We observe that rare variable names in a source code unnecessarily extend input sequence length, thus reducing effective context length. We tried to use some transformer modifications such as Reformer (Kitaev et al., 2020) to reduce inference time but the quality drop was very high.

Here we propose a simple idea of replacing a rare variable name with a placeholder (`varK`, where K is the variable index number) if its frequency is less than a certain threshold. Also, we should note, that by such replacement the language modeling task becomes a bit easier. Since there is no need to remember complex variable names and the model can concentrate on predicting more useful token sequences.

Proposed substitution increases quality and speed not only because of the context size. It is impossible to get a long name variable from the model output because there is a limit on the number of generation iterations. While such transformation allows us to generate a variable of any length.

3.3 Prefix Generation

We observe some discrepancy between training objective and model usage cases. Usually, the user can improve completion results by typing in several first characters of the desired token. The problem is that during inference user may invoke an autocompletion service, while the pointer is still in the middle of the BPE token of the desired output. So, at the training stage the tokenization is determined, while during inference it can take an arbitrary form. When the word is typed in by the user, its prefixes may be decomposed into BPE tokens in several different ways. For example, if a user wants to get the variable `maxDf` consisting of `max` and `df` BPE tokens, then the typed `m` can lead only to an unlikely sequence `m`, `ax`, `df`.

We try to work around this issue by utilizing token prefixes. To incorporate signal from the prefix, we propose to roll the pointer back to the start of the program token and to utilize only those BPE tokens that match our prefix during beam search. Searching tokens with the right prefix is computationally expensive ($O(D)$ for each call, D is a dictionary size). To overcome the computational cost we use the trie data structure to store all the BPE tokens ($O(m)$ for each call, m is the maximum length of the BPE token in the dictionary).

3.4 Beam Search with Early Stopping

We investigated full-line code completion setting, where we try to predict a sequence of program tokens till the end of the line. We selected the average number of correct program tokens predicted as our quality metric. We found out, that if we restrict model size and use regular language modeling objective, the model starts to hallucinate after 1-2 program tokens. So we decided to restrict our in ference only to 1 program token, introducing early stopping into the beam search routine.

It is easy to understand if a generated sequence is exhausted in a single token completion task. The lexer is applied to extract program tokens after each beam search iteration. If at some point the lexer output contains more than one program token, the generation process is stopped for the current sequence. We also stop the beam search if we have already obtained k complete tokens, where k is a hyperparameter. It helps to accelerate the inference and has nearly no negative effect on model quality.

3.5 Distillation

Distillation is a model compression procedure in which a student model is trained to match the outputs of a large pre-trained teacher model. Some works (Bucila et al., 2006; Hinton et al., 2015) show that distilled model can perform even better than a trained from scratch model with the same architecture and the same amount of parameters.

For distillation, we use the cross entropy loss along with the KL divergence between the student and teacher outputs (Equation 3, where p_s is a student model, p_t is a teacher model, and α is hyperparameter to balance losses).

$$q(x,t) = -(1-\alpha)\log p_s(x_t|x_{<t}) + \\ + \alpha\, KL\left(p_s(x_t|x_{<t}) \mid\mid p_t(x_t|x_{<t})\right) \quad (2)$$

$$\mathcal{L}_{dist} = \sum_t q(x,t) \rightarrow \min \quad (3)$$

4 Dataset

The dataset used for the model training consists of 500k R Markdown files (Rmd). Non-code information is erased from each file and the rest of the text is transformed into a script. Additionally, in one of the experiments we use a larger dataset that contains more than 4kk with both R and Rmd files.

The evaluation dataset was collected from the Github open-source projects and consists of 35k examples from the 9k R files. There is an issue with the using of the open-source project codes for the evaluation. It is very likely for the training and the test sets to intersect. A lot of repositories have forks with minimal differences and it is very hard to distinguish them from the source one. That is why we evaluate most of our models on R files only while training on Rmd files to avoid encountering the training samples in the test set.

Some papers investigate autocompletion behaviour on real-world autocompletion logs. Aye et al. (2020) showed that autocompletion models trained as language models on an unlabelled corpus perform much worse on the real-world logs than models trained on a logs dataset initially. Hellendoorn et al. (2019) showed a difference in the distributions of the completed tokens between the real completion events and the synthetic evaluation datasets.

after_operator_$	2158
after_operator_%>%	1493
after_operator_->	43
after_operator_::	1024
after_operator_<-	3748
after_operator_=	4488
c_key_argument	598
c_positional_argument	1776
f_key_argument	8920
f_positional_argument	6730
library	748
new_line_variable	1774
new_line_function	1113
with prefix	15470
without prefix	19143

Table 1: Dataset group sizes

Not having the real logs available, we decided to divide our synthetic evaluation dataset into several groups. It is useful to validate a model behaviour on different autocompletion contexts. This way, the model can be fine-tuned to improve quality in concrete autocompletion situations, such as a package import or a function call completion. Firstly, we divide the dataset into prefix and non-prefix groups. The last program token is always incomplete in the prefix group. Also, we divide our examples into groups by the usage context. For example, there is a group with the filling of the function arguments and a group with new variables declaration.

The first type of dataset groups corresponds to completion events following the concrete operators (`$`, `%>%`, `->`, `::` `<-`, `=`). Another type covers autocompletion events during the positional or keyword arguments completion in vectors or functions. The next one consists of packages import usage contexts. The last one corresponds to the completion of a variable or a function name at the start of the new line.

5 Experiments

The code completion task may be considered a ranking problem. We use mean reciprocal rank score (MRR) and mean Recall@5 score for evaluation in our experiments. There is only one relevant element a in the autocompletion task and with search results denoted as s the formulas can be written as follows.

$$RR(a,s) = \begin{cases} i^{-1}, & \text{if } s_i = a \\ 0, & \text{if } a \notin s \end{cases}$$

$$Recall@k(a,s) = \sum_{i=1}^{k} \mathbb{I}[a = s_i]$$

5.1 Implementation Details

Our aim is to build a model light enough to run smoothly on an average laptop. We evaluate our models on a laptop equipped with Intel Core i7 with 6 cores and 16 GB RAM. The average time for the single autocompletion event should be close to 100ms and RAM consumption should not exceed 400MB.

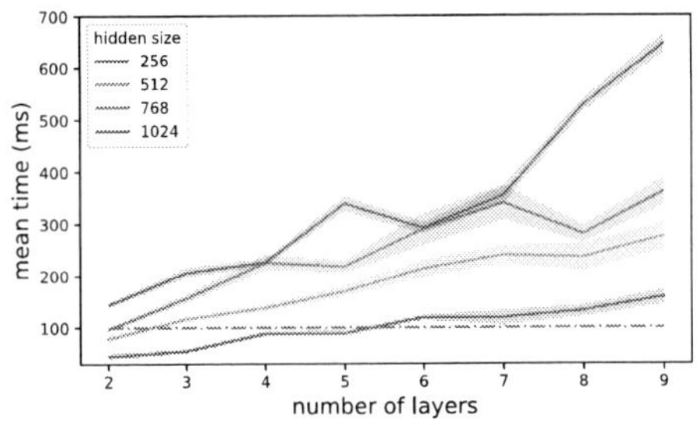

Figure 1: Mean inference time over 50k objects for different model parameters

Figure 1 presents average inference times for our model with all the proposed modifications. We keep the number of heads = 4 and vary hidden size and number of layers. It can be seen that the model with the hidden size = 256 and number of layers = 4 is the most complicated model that still satisfies the performance requirements.

5.2 Quality and Inference Speed

In this experiment, we evaluate each of our proposed modifications from the section 3. We apply modifications one by one and measure metrics and mean inference time for each of them. We use a transformer model with parameters from the previous experiment (hidden size = 256, heads amount = 4, number of layers = 4) as the baseline. For all experiments, we use Adam (Kingma and Ba, 2017) optimizer with the default parameters, cosine annealing learning rate scheduler (Smith and Topin, 2018) with upper learning rate boundary 5e-3 and gradient norm clipping by 10.

The results show that without the prefix generation modification the model is unable to take advantage of the given prefixes. It should be noted that almost 45% of the examples from the evaluation dataset contain unfinished tokens with a given prefix. Additional manipulations with the prefix slow down the model but it is compensated by the following two modifications. Variable name substitution during the prepossessing leads to both quality improvement and inference speed up. Generation early stopping procedure accelerates the inference without any ranking drawback.

	MRR	Recall@5	time
baseline	0.319	0.364	150 ms
+ prefix generation	0.64	0.709	195 ms
+ variable replacing	0.673	0.748	183 ms
+ BS early stopping	0.676	0.751	98 ms

Table 2: Model modifications performance

5.3 Big Dataset Effect

One of the standard methods to improve model performance in data science is to collect more data. As we mentioned before, we can not guarantee total fairness of the evaluation process in this setup, but we try to make sure that all the training examples are removed from the test set by eliminating possible duplicates.

	MRR	Recall@5
l4 s256	0.676	0.751
l6 s1024	0.683	0.751
+ more data	0.761	0.815
+ distillation	0.701	0.767

Table 3: Increasing dataset size and distillation effects

We consider multiple types of models in this experiment. The first one is the best model from experiment 5.2. The second experiment is similar to the first one but consists of six layers instead of four and has hidden size of 1024 instead of 256. The third experiment has the same architecture as the second one and is trained on a larger training set.

	w/o prefix		with prefix		both	
	MRR	Recall@5	MRR	Recall@5	MRR	Recall@5
after_operator_$	0.596	0.669	0.727	0.779	0.656	0.719
after_operator_%>%	0.566	0.714	0.840	0.895	0.702	0.804
after_operator_->	0.218	0.276	0.214	0.286	0.217	0.279
after_operator_::	0.614	0.716	0.798	0.858	0.709	0.789
after_operator_<-	0.563	0.659	0.787	0.849	0.666	0.746
after_operator_=	0.624	0.707	0.765	0.793	0.682	0.743
c_key_argument	0.659	0.706	0.796	0.824	0.719	0.758
c_positional_argument	0.752	0.820	0.815	0.846	0.778	0.831
f_key_argument	0.713	0.784	0.840	0.876	0.771	0.826
f_positional_argument	0.719	0.812	0.803	0.852	0.755	0.829
library	0.183	0.299	0.775	0.870	0.463	0.570
new_line_function	0.586	0.704	0.676	0.771	0.630	0.737
new_line_variable	0.274	0.316	0.329	0.377	0.299	0.344

Table 4: Distilled model performance on separate groups. Rows correspond to autocompletion contexts. Results for no prefix subset, prefix subset, and entire dataset are split into columns.

We apply Adaptive Softmax (Grave et al., 2017) during the first training iterations to speed up the training process. The fourth experiment is a result of distillation of the third one into the model with the architecture from the first experiment.

As we see from the results (Table 3) both increasing training set size and distillation have positive effect on the metrics. The distilled model outperforms all the models trained on a small dataset, even the more complicated ones.

5.4 Error Interpretation

Table 4 shows the distilled model performance on different parts of the evaluation dataset. In general, the additional prefix information allows achieving a higher score. Groups related to function arguments and vector content have the highest MRR score. It is an interesting observation since the vector content is eliminated during the preprocessing step. It seems that vector argument filling is very close to function argument filling semantically and the model is able to perform well in this situation without any relevant training samples.

The additional prefix information is very important for a `library` group. Library calls are usually located at the start of the program. If there is no last token prefix then the only reasonable model behaviour is to predict the most common completion.

Autocompletion usage after the <− operator means that we want to get a variable computation statement based on a variable name. In opposite, usage after the −> means that we want to get a variable name based on given computations. Corresponding groups at the table show that we are much better at the first one completion group. It makes sense as the user has no limits in the variable name design. Another reason for the low quality for the `after_operator_->` is a low amount of examples for this operator in the training data. That is why the quality for the `new_line_variable group` is better even though the task is harder.

6 Conclusions

In this work, we present a model for the R programming language completion. We introduced simple but effective techniques, which can improve a code completion quality, while not affecting the model architecture or the training objective. Thus, these techniques can be easily combined with other works in the field and any dynamic programming language. We also present an evaluation dataset for the R programming language containing different autocompletion contexts. The diversity of our dataset provides a robust estimation.

References

Uri Alon, Roy Sadaka, Omer Levy, and Eran Yahav. 2019. Structural language models for any-code generation. *CoRR*, abs/1910.00577.

Gareth Ari Aye, Seohyun Kim, and Hongyu Li. 2020. Learning autocompletion from real-world datasets.

Tom B. Brown, Benjamin Mann, Nick Ryder, Melanie

Subbiah, Jared Kaplan, Prafulla Dhariwal, Arvind Neelakantan, Pranav Shyam, Girish Sastry, Amanda Askell, Sandhini Agarwal, Ariel Herbert-Voss, Gretchen Krueger, Tom Henighan, Rewon Child, Aditya Ramesh, Daniel M. Ziegler, Jeffrey Wu, Clemens Winter, Christopher Hesse, Mark Chen, Eric Sigler, Mateusz Litwin, Scott Gray, Benjamin Chess, Jack Clark, Christopher Berner, Sam McCandlish, Alec Radford, Ilya Sutskever, and Dario Amodei. 2020. Language models are few-shot learners.

Marcel Bruch, Martin Monperrus, and Mira Mezini. 2009. Learning from examples to improve code completion systems. pages 213–222.

Cristian Bucila, Rich Caruana, and Alexandru Niculescu-Mizil. 2006. Model compression. In *KDD*, pages 535–541. ACM.

Edouard Grave, Armand Joulin, Moustapha Cissé, David Grangier, and Hervé Jégou. 2017. Efficient softmax approximation for gpus.

Vincent J. Hellendoorn, Sebastian Proksch, Harald C. Gall, and Alberto Bacchelli. 2019. When code completion fails: a case study on real-world completions. In *Proceedings of the 41st International Conference on Software Engineering, ICSE 2019, Montreal, QC, Canada, May 25-31, 2019*, pages 960–970. IEEE / ACM.

Geoffrey Hinton, Oriol Vinyals, and Jeff Dean. 2015. Distilling the knowledge in a neural network.

Nitish Shirish Keskar, Bryan McCann, Lav R. Varshney, Caiming Xiong, and Richard Socher. 2019. CTRL: A conditional transformer language model for controllable generation. *CoRR*, abs/1909.05858.

Diederik P. Kingma and Jimmy Ba. 2017. Adam: A method for stochastic optimization.

Nikita Kitaev, Łukasz Kaiser, and Anselm Levskaya. 2020. Reformer: The efficient transformer.

Jian Li, Yue Wang, Irwin King, and Michael R. Lyu. 2017. Code completion with neural attention and pointer networks. *CoRR*, abs/1711.09573.

Fang Liu, Ge Li, Yunfei Zhao, and Zhi Jin. 2020. Multitask learning based pre-trained language model for code completion.

Alec Radford, Jeffrey Wu, Rewon Child, David Luan, Dario Amodei, and Ilya Sutskever. 2019. Language models are unsupervised multitask learners. *OpenAI blog*, 1(8):9.

Rico Sennrich, Barry Haddow, and Alexandra Birch. 2015. Neural machine translation of rare words with subword units. *arXiv preprint arXiv:1508.07909*

Nicholas McKay Shelley. 2014. Autocompletion without static typing.

Leslie N. Smith and Nicholay Topin. 2018. Super-convergence: Very fast training of neural networks using large learning rates.

Zhaopeng Tu, Zhendong Su, and Premkumar Devanbu. 2014. On the localness of software. In *Proceedings of the 22nd ACM SIGSOFT International Symposium on Foundations of Software Engineering*, FSE 2014, page 269–280, New York, NY, USA. Association for Computing Machinery.

CoTexT: Multi-task Learning with Code-Text Transformer

Long Phan[1], Hieu Tran[2], Daniel Le[1], Hieu Nguyen[1], James Anibal[1], Alec Peltekian[1], and Yanfang Ye[1]

[1]Case Western Reserve University, Ohio, USA
[2]University of Science, VNU-HCM, Vietnam
{lnp26, yxy1032}@case.edu

Abstract

We present CoTexT, a pre-trained, transformer-based encoder-decoder model that learns the representative context between natural language (NL) and programming language (PL). Using self-supervision, CoTexT is pre-trained on large programming language corpora to learn a general understanding of language and code. CoTexT supports downstream NL-PL tasks such as code summarizing/documentation, code generation, defect detection, and code debugging. We train CoTexT on different combinations of available PL corpus including both "bimodal" and "unimodal" data. Here, bimodal data is the combination of text and corresponding code snippets, whereas unimodal data is merely code snippets. We first evaluate CoTexT with multi-task learning: we perform Code Summarization on 6 different programming languages and Code Refinement on both small and medium size featured in the CodeXGLUE dataset. We further conduct extensive experiments to investigate CoTexT on other tasks within the CodeXGlue dataset, including Code Generation and Defect Detection. We consistently achieve SOTA results in these tasks, demonstrating the versatility of our models.

1 Introduction

In recent years, pre-trained language models (LM) have played a crucial role in the development of many natural language processing (NLP) systems. Before the emergence of large LMs, traditional word embedding gives each word/token a global representation. Large pre-trained models such as ELMo (Peters et al., 2018), GPT (Brown et al., 2020), BERT (Devlin et al., 2018), and XLNet (Yang et al., 2020) can derive contextualized word vector representations from large corpora. These methods can learn generalized representations of language and have significantly improved a broad range of downstream NLP tasks. These LMs make use of learning objectives such as Masked Language Modeling (MLM) (Devlin et al., 2018) where random tokens in a sequence are masked and the model predicts the original tokens to learn the context. The success of pre-trained models in NLP has created a path for domain-specific pre-trained LMs, such as BioBERT (Lee et al., 2019a) on biomedical text, or TaBERT (Yin et al., 2020) on NL text and tabular data.

We introduce CoTexT (Code and Text Transfer Transformer), a pre-trained model for both natural language (NL) and programming language (PL) such as Java, Python, Javascript, PHP, etc. CoTexT follows the encoder-decoder architecture proposed by (Vaswani et al., 2017) with attention mechanisms. We then adapt the model to match T5 framework proposed by (Raffel et al., 2019). We test CoTexT by performing exhaustive experiments on multi-task learning of multiple programming languages and other related tasks.

We train CoTexT using large programming language corpora containing multiple programming languages (including Java, Python, JavaScript, Ruby, etc.). Here, we test different combinations of unimodal and bimodal data to produce the best result for each downstream task. We then fine-tune CoTexT on four CodeXGLUE tasks (Lu et al., 2021) including CodeSummarization, CodeGeneration, Defect Detection and Code Refinement (small and medium dataset). Results show that we achieve state-of-the-art values for each of the four tasks. We found that CoTexT outperforms current SOTA models such as CodeBERT (Feng et al., 2020) and PLBART (Ahmad et al., 2021a).

In this paper we offer the following contribution:

- Three different versions of CoTexT that achieve state-of-the-art on the CodeXGLUE's CodeSummarization, CodeGeneration, Defect

Proceedings of the 1st Workshop on Natural Language Processing for Programming (NLP4Prog 2021), pages 40–47
August 1–6, 2021. ©2021 Association for Computational Linguistics

Detection and Code Refinement (small and medium dataset) tasks. We publicize our CoTexT pre-trained checkpoints and related source code available for future studies and improvements.

2 Related Work

Recent work on domain adaptation of BERT show improvements compared to the general BERT model. BioBERT (Lee et al., 2019b) is further trained from $\text{BERT}_{\text{BASE}}$ on biomedical articles such as PubMed abstracts and PMC articles. Similarly, SciBERT (Beltagy et al., 2019) is trained on the full text of biomedical and computer science papers. The experimental results of these models on domain-specific datasets show the enhanced performance compared to $\text{BERT}_{\text{BASE}}$.

Relating specfically to our work, CodeBERT is (Feng et al., 2020) trained on bimodal data of NL-PL pairs. This strategy allows CodeBERT to learn general-purpose representations of both natural language and programming language. GraphCodeBERT (Guo et al., 2021) is an extension of CodeBERT that moves beyond syntactic-level structure and uses data flow in the pre-training stage to capture the semantic-level structure of code. More recently, PLBART (Ahmad et al., 2021b) is a pre-trained sequence-to-sequence model for NL and PL. Through denoising autoencoding, this model can perform well on NL-PL understanding and generation tasks.

3 CoTexT

3.1 Vocabulary

Following the example of T5 (Raffel et al., 2019), we use the Sentence Piece Unsupervised Text Tokenizer proposed by (Kudo and Richardson, 2018). The Sentence Piece model extracts the sub-words that contain the semantic context of a sequence. We employ Sentence Piece as a vocabulary model for all of our contributed CoTexT models. However, the special tokens used in code (such as "[", "{", "$", etc) are out-of-vocab for the SentencePiece model [1]. These tokens have a crucial representative context in programming languages. Therefore, to enhance the robustness of the model, we encode all of these missing tokens into a natural language representation during both self-supervised and supervised training.

[1] https://github.com/google/sentencepiece

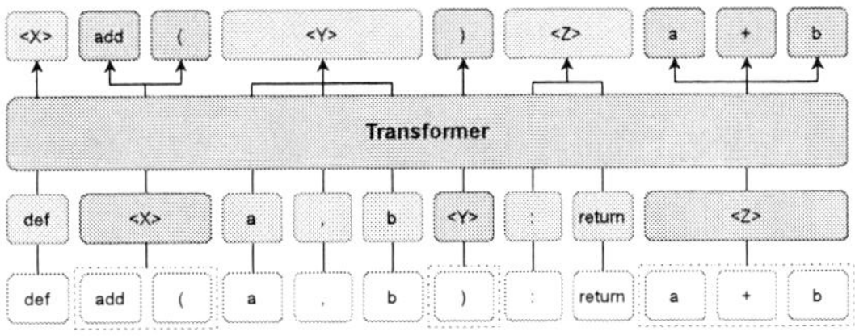

Figure 1: An illustration about Fill-in-the-blank objective

3.2 Pre-training CoTexT

We train CoTexT on both bimodal and unimodal data. Bimodal data contains both code snippets and the corresponding natural text in each sequence, while unimodal data contains only the sequence of code. We use two main datasets during self-supervised training: **CodeSearchNet Corpus Collection** (Husain et al., 2020) and **GitHub Repositories**[2] data. The combinations of corpus used to train CoTexT are listed in Table 1. To save both time and computing resources, we initialized the checkpoints from the original T5 that was trained on the C4 corpus. (Raffel et al., 2019).

3.2.1 CodeSearchNet Corpus Collection

CodeSearchNet Corpus (Husain et al., 2020) contains coded functions from open-source non-forked Github repositories. This dataset spans 6 coding languages (Python, Java, Javascript, PHP, Ruby, Go), which facilitates multi-task learning. CodeSearchNet also contains a natural language description for each function. For bimodal data, we simply concatenate the natural language snippet with the corresponding code snippet to create one input sequence. These data are then processed as described in 3.1.

3.2.2 GitHub repositories

We download a large collection of Java and Python functions from the GitHub repositories dataset available on Google BigQuery. These Java and Python functions are then extracted and the natural language descriptions are obtained using the pre-processing pipeline from (Lachaux et al., 2020). These datapoints also run through a pipeline to replace special tokens (as described in 3.1).

3.3 Input/Output Representations

CoTexT converts all NLP problems into a text-to-text format. This means that during both self-

[2] https://console.cloud.google.com/marketplace/details/github/github-repos

Table 1: Pre-training CoTexT on different combinations of natural language and programming language copora

Model	N-modal	Corpus combination
T5	NL	C4
CoTexT (1-CC)	PL	**C**4 + **C**odeSearchNet
CoTexT (2-CC)	NL-PL	**C**4 + **C**odeSearchNet
CoTexT (1-CCG)	PL	**C**4 + **C**odeSearchNet + **G**ithub Repos

supervised pre-training and supervised training, we use an input sequence and a target sequence. For the bimodal model, we concatenate a sequence of natural language text and the corresponding sequence of programming language text as an input. For the unimodal model, we simply use each coded function as an input sequence. During self-supervised training, spans of the input sequence are randomly masked and the target sequence (Raffel et al., 2019) is formed as the concatenation of the same sentinel tokens and the real masked spans/tokens.

3.4 Model Architecture

CoTexT follows the sequence-to-sequence encoder-decoder architecture proposed by (Vaswani et al., 2017). We initialize the Base T5 model released by (Raffel et al., 2019) which has 220 million parameters. We train the model with a 0.001 learning rate and an input/target length of 1024. With the provided TPU v2-8 on Google Colab, we train with the recommended setting of model parallelism 2 and batch size 128.

3.5 Multi-task Learning

The model is trained with maximum likelihood objective (that is using "teacher forcing" (Williams and Zipser, 1989)) regardless of the text-code or code-text tasks. Therefore, for CoTexT, we leverage the potential for Multi-Task learning (Raffel et al., 2019) to complete both text-code and code-text generation on CodeSummarization and Code Refinement tasks. To specify the task our model should perform, we simply add a task-specific prefix to the input sequence. For example, when fine-tuning of the CodeSummarization task for each programming language, we simply prepend a prefix for each PL name (i.e., Java) to the input sequence.

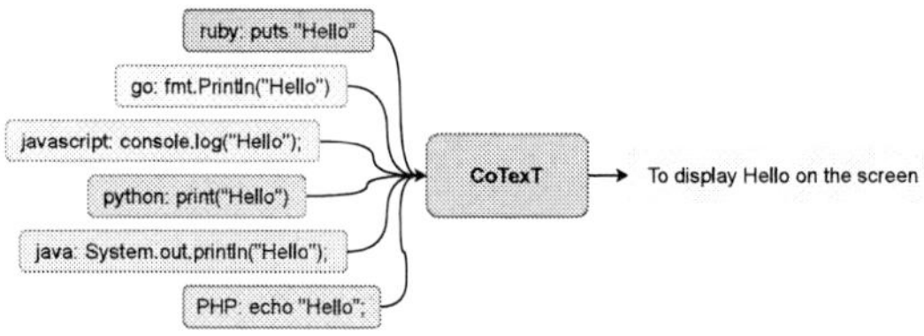

Figure 2: An illustration about Multi-task learning

4 Experiments

In this section, we will first describe the benchmark dataset for code intelligence CodeXGLUE, then we will explain the experimental setup on the tasks we perform and discuss the results of each task. The evaluation datasets are summarized in Table 3.

4.1 CodeXGLUE

General Language Understanding Evaluation benchmark for CODE (CodeXGLUE) (Lu et al., 2021) is a benchmark dataset to facilitate machine learning studies on code understanding and code generation problems. This dataset includes a collection of code intelligence tasks (both classification and generation), a platform for model evaluation, and a leaderboard for comparison. CodeXGLUE has 10 code intelligence tasks including code-text, text-code, code-code, and text-text scenarios. For CoTexT, we focus on Code Summarization, Code Generation, Code Refinement, and Defect Detection tasks.

4.2 Evaluation Tasks

We evaluate our programming language and natural language generation tasks on TPU v2-8 with the settings from the original T5 model (Raffel et al., 2019). The input length and target length for each task are described in Table 2.

4.2.1 Code Summarization

For Code Summarization, the objective is to generate a natural language description for a given code snippet. The task includes a CodeSearchNet dataset (Husain et al., 2019) with 6 different programming languages: Python, Java, Javascript, PHP, Ruby, Go. The data comes from public open-source non-fork GitHub repositories and the annotations are ex-

Table 2: The input and target sequence length settings for each self-supervised learning, code summarization, code generation, code refinement, and defect detection task

Task	Dataset	Task Type	Input Length	Target Length
Self-supervised Learning	CodSearchNet Corpus		1024	1024
	GitHub Repositories		1024	1024
Code Summarization	CodeSearchNet	Multi-Task	512	512
Code Generation	CONCODE	Single-Task	256	256
Code Refinement	$\text{Bugs2Fix}_{\text{small}}$ $\text{Bugs2Fix}_{\text{medium}}$	Multi-Task	512	512
Defect Detection	Devign	Single-Task	1024	5

tracted from function documentation as described in (Husain et al., 2019).

4.2.2 Code Generation

Text-to-Code Generation aims to generate a coded function given a natural language description. This task is completed using the CONCODE dataset (Iyer et al., 2018), a well-known dataset for Java language generation. Within the dataset, there are tuples which contain a natural language description, code environments, ad code snippets. The goal is to generate the correct Java function from the natural language description in the form of Javadoc-style method comments.

4.2.3 Code Refinement

Code Refinement, or Code Repair, aims to automatically correct bugs in Java code. We used the Bug2Fix corpus released by CodeXGLUE (Lu et al., 2021), which divides the task into 2 subsets: SMALL and MEDIUM The small dataset includes only Java code functions with fewer than 50 tokens. The medium dataset includes functions with 50-100 tokens.

4.2.4 Defect Detection

For Defect Detection tasks, we attempt to classify whether a PL snippet contains vulnerabilities that could lead to damaging outcomes such as resource leaks or DoS attacks. The task uses the Devign dataset (Zhou et al., 2019), which contains C programming language from open-source projects. This dataset is labeled based on security-related commits. For details on the annotation process, refer to (Zhou et al., 2019).

4.3 Experimental Setup

4.3.1 Baselines

We compare our model with some well-known pre-trained models:

- CodeGPT, CodeGPT-adapted are based on the architecture and training objective of GPT-2 (Budzianowski and Vulic, 2019). CodeGPT is pre-trained from scratch on CodeSearchNet dataset (Lu et al., 2021) while CodeGPT-adapted learns this dataset starting from the GPT-2 checkpoint.
- CodeBERT (Feng et al., 2020) employs the same architecture as RoBERTa (Liu et al., 2020) but aims to minimize the combined loss from masked language modeling and replaced token detection.
- PLBART (Ahmad et al., 2021b) is a Transformer-based model. BART (Lewis et al., 2019) is trained on PL corpora using three learning strategies: token masking, token deletion, and token infilling.

4.3.2 Performance Metrics

- BLEU (Papineni et al., 2002) is an algorithm which performs automatic evaluation of machine-translated text. This method calculates the n-gram similarity of a candidate translation compared to a set of reference texts. Similar to (Feng et al., 2020) and (Ahmad et al., 2021b), we use smooth BLEU-4 score (**?**) for Code Summarization and corpus-level BLEU score for all remaining tasks.
- CodeBLEU (Ren et al., 2020) is designed to consider syntactic and semantic features of

Table 3: Data statistics about Code Intelligence datasets

Category	Task	Dataset	Size			Language
			Train	Val	Test	
Code-Text	Code Summarization (Lu et al., 2021)	CodeSearchNet	164K	5.1K	10.9K	Java
			58K	3.8K	3.2K	Javascript
			251K	13.9K	14.9K	Python
			241K	12.9K	14K	PHP
			167K	7.3K	8.1K	Go
			24K	1.4K	1.2K	Ruby
Code-Code	Defect Detection (Zhou et al., 2019)	Devign	21K	2.7K	2.7K	C
	Code Refinement (Lu et al., 2021)	$\text{Bugs2Fix}_{\text{small}}$	46K	5.8K	5.8K	Java
		$\text{Bugs2Fix}_{\text{medium}}$	52K	6.5K	6.5K	
Text-Code	Code Generation (Iyer et al., 2018)	CONCODE	100K	2K	2K	Java

codes based on the abstract syntax tree and the data flow structure.

- Accuracy is the ratio of the number of generated sequences that harmonise the reference to the total number of observations.

5 Results

5.1 Multi-Task Learning

We first report the result of CoTexT in Multi-Task Learning tasks including Code Summarization and Code Refinement.

5.1.1 Code Summarization

For the Code Summarization task, we perform Multi-Task Learning by using the T5 framework (Raffel et al., 2019) to finetune CoTexT on 6 diferent programming language (Ruby, Javascript, Go, Python, Java, and PHP). The results of the Code Summarization task are shown in Table 5.

First, we observe that the base T5, which is pre-trained only on the general domain corpus (C4), is effective on this task. In fact, base T5 achieves higher overall results on the BLEU-4 metric compared to all other related models on the CodeXGLUE leaderboard. This shows the importance of domain-specific T5 models, which we expect to achieve superior results compared to base T5.

We further observe that CoTexT achieves state-of-the-art (SOTA) on the overall score, the Python-specific score, the Java-specific score, and the Go-specific score. While CoTexT does not significantly outperform other pre-trained models, we observe that CoTexT achieves SOTA on two very common programming languages (Python and Java) while still obtaining competitive results on other programming languages. We attribute this result to the large amount of training data for Python and Java compared to the other languages (training size described in Table 3). Based on this result, CoTeXT has the potential to further surpass competitor models as more training data becomes availible.

5.1.2 Code Refinement

We also tested CoTexT by performing multi-task learning for Code Refinement. In this case, both the small and medium test sets have a task registry with respective prefix prepending to the input sequence.

The Code Refinement results of each model are shown in Table 6. For this task, the base T5, which is pre-trained only on natural language text, does not perform well compared to other transformer-based models. Yet, after the training on a large programming language corpus, the result from CoTexT improves significantly on all metrics for both small and medium test sets. CoTexT achieves SOTA for all metrics on the small test set and on the accuracy metric for the medium test set.

5.2 Single-Task Learning

In addition to multi-task learning, we also evaluate CoTexT performance single-task learning with

Table 4: Test result on Code Generation task

Model	Text2Code Generation		
	EM	BLEU	CodeBLEU
PLBART	18.75	<u>36.69</u>	38.52
CodeGPT-adapted	20.10	32.79	35.98
CodeGPT	18.25	28.69	32.71
T5	18.65	32.74	35.95
CoText (1-CCG)	19.45	35.40	38.47
CoText (2-CC)	<u>20.10</u>	36.51	<u>39.49</u>
CoText (1-CC)	**20.10**	**37.40**	**40.14**

Notes: The best scores are in bold and second best scores are underlined. The baseline scores were obtained from the CodeXGLUE's Leaderboard (https://microsoft.github.io/CodeXGLUE/)

Table 5: Test result on Code Summarization task

Model	All	Ruby	Javascript	Go	Python	Java	PHP
RoBERTa	16.57	11.17	11.90	17.72	18.14	16.47	24.02
CodeBERT	17.83	12.16	14.90	18.07	19.06	17.65	**25.16**
PLBART	18.32	**14.11**	**15.56**	18.91	19.3	18.45	23.58
T5	18.35	14.18	14.57	<u>19.17</u>	19.26	18.35	24.59
CoTexT (1-CCG)	18.00	13.23	14.75	18.95	19.35	18.75	22.97
CoTexT (2-CC)	<u>18.38</u>	13.07	14.77	**19.37**	<u>19.52</u>	**19.1**	24.47
CoTexT (1-CC)	**18.55**	<u>14.02</u>	<u>14.96</u>	18.86	**19.73**	<u>19.06</u>	<u>24.58</u>

Notes: The best scores are in bold and second best scores are underlined. The baseline scores were obtained from the CodeXGLUE's Leaderboard (https://microsoft.github.io/CodeXGLUE/)

Table 6: Test result on Code Refinement task

Model	Small test set			Medium test set		
	BLEU	Acc(%)	CodeBLEU	BLEU	Acc(%)	CodeBLEU
Transformer	77.21	14.70	73.31	<u>89.25</u>	3.70	81.72
CodeBERT	77.42	16.40	75.58	**91.07**	5.16	**87.52**
PLBART	77.02	19.21	/	88.5	8.98	/
T5	74.94	15.3	75.85	88.28	4.11	85.61
CoTexT (1-CCG)	76.87	20.39	<u>77.34</u>	88.58	12.88	<u>86.05</u>
CoTexT (2-CC)	<u>77.28</u>	**21.58**	**77.38**	88.68	<u>13.03</u>	84.41
CoTexT (1-CC)	**77.79**	<u>21.03</u>	76.15	88.4	**13.11**	85.83

Notes: The best scores are in bold and second best scores are underlined. The baseline scores were obtained from the CodeXGLUE's Leaderboard (https://microsoft.github.io/CodeXGLUE/)

Table 7: Test result on Defect Detection task

Model	Accuracy
RoBERTa	61.05
CodeBERT	62.08
PLBART	63.18
T5	61.93
CoTexT (1-CCG)	**66.62**
CoTexT (2-CC)	64.49
CoTexT (1-CC)	<u>65.99</u>

Notes: The best scores are in bold and second best scores are underlined. The baseline scores were obtained from the CodeXGLUE's Leaderboard (https://microsoft.github.io/CodeXGLUE/)

a Code Generation Task and a classification task relating to Defect Detection.

5.2.1 Code Generation

In Table 4, we reported our results for the Code Generation task wherein natural language is translated into Java code. The result shows that our proposed model achieves SOTA results based on 3 metrics: Exact Match (EM), BLEU, and CodeBLEU. For each individual metric, CoTexT has only slightly outperformed other models (e.g both CoTexT and CodeGPT-adapted achieve 20.10 for EM). However, our model is consistently superior across the 3 metrics. Prior to CoTexT, CodeGPT-adapted was SOTA for the EM metric and PLBART was SOTA for the BLUE/CodeBLUE metrics. From this result, we infer that CoTexT has the best overall performance on this task and has great potential in the area of code generation.

5.2.2 Defect Detection

The Defect Detection results are shown in Table 7. Specifically, CoText outperforms the previous SOTA model (PLBART) by 3.44%. For this task, extra training on a large programming corpus allows CoTexT to outperform all other models and achieve SOTA results. The Defect Detection dataset consists of code written in the C programming language, which is not contained in our training data. Our model has a strong understanding of similar languages, and is thus able to perform Defect Detection in C with improved results compared to competitor models.

6 Conclusion

In this manuscript, we introduced CoTexT, a pre-trained language representation for both programming language and natural language. CoTexT focused on text-code and code-text understanding and generating. Leveraging the T5 framework (Raffel et al., 2019), we showed that pre-training on a large programming language corpus is effective for a diverse array of tasks within the natural language and programming language domain. CoTexT achieves state-of-the-art results on 4 CodeXGLUE code intelligence tasks: Code Summarization, Code Generation, Code Refinement, and Code Detection. For future work, we plan to test CoTexT on a broader range of programming language and natural language generation tasks, such as autocompletion or code translation.

References

Wasi Uddin Ahmad, Saikat Chakraborty, Baishakhi Ray, and Kai-Wei Chang. 2021a. Unified pre-training for program understanding and generation.

Wasi Uddin Ahmad, Saikat Chakraborty, Baishakhi Ray, and Kai-Wei Chang. 2021b. Unified pre-training for program understanding and generation. In *Proceedings of the 2021 Conference of the North American Chapter of the Association for Computational Linguistics*.

Iz Beltagy, Arman Cohan, and Kyle Lo. 2019. Scibert: Pretrained contextualized embeddings for scientific text. *CoRR*, abs/1903.10676.

Tom B. Brown, Benjamin Mann, Nick Ryder, Melanie Subbiah, Jared Kaplan, Prafulla Dhariwal, Arvind Neelakantan, Pranav Shyam, Girish Sastry, Amanda Askell, Sandhini Agarwal, Ariel Herbert-Voss, Gretchen Krueger, Tom Henighan, Rewon Child, Aditya Ramesh, Daniel M. Ziegler, Jeffrey Wu, Clemens Winter, Christopher Hesse, Mark Chen, Eric Sigler, Mateusz Litwin, Scott Gray, Benjamin Chess, Jack Clark, Christopher Berner, Sam McCandlish, Alec Radford, Ilya Sutskever, and Dario Amodei. 2020. Language models are few-shot learners.

Pawel Budzianowski and Ivan Vulic. 2019. Hello, it's GPT-2 - how can I help you? towards the use of pre-trained language models for task-oriented dialogue systems. *CoRR*, abs/1907.05774.

Jacob Devlin, Ming-Wei Chang, Kenton Lee, and Kristina Toutanova. 2018. BERT: pre-training of deep bidirectional transformers for language understanding. *CoRR*, abs/1810.04805.

Zhangyin Feng, Daya Guo, Duyu Tang, Nan Duan, Xiaocheng Feng, Ming Gong, Linjun Shou, Bing Qin,

Ting Liu, Daxin Jiang, and Ming Zhou. 2020. Codebert: A pre-trained model for programming and natural languages. *CoRR*, abs/2002.08155.

Daya Guo, Shuo Ren, Shuai Lu, Zhangyin Feng, Duyu Tang, Shujie LIU, Long Zhou, Nan Duan, Alexey Svyatkovskiy, Shengyu Fu, Michele Tufano, Shao Kun Deng, Colin Clement, Dawn Drain, Neel Sundaresan, Jian Yin, Daxin Jiang, and Ming Zhou. 2021. Graphcode{bert}: Pre-training code representations with data flow. In *International Conference on Learning Representations*.

Hamel Husain, Ho-Hsiang Wu, Tiferet Gazit, Miltiadis Allamanis, and Marc Brockschmidt. 2019. Codesearchnet challenge: Evaluating the state of semantic code search. *CoRR*, abs/1909.09436.

Hamel Husain, Ho-Hsiang Wu, Tiferet Gazit, Miltiadis Allamanis, and Marc Brockschmidt. 2020. Codesearchnet challenge: Evaluating the state of semantic code search.

Srinivasan Iyer, Ioannis Konstas, Alvin Cheung, and Luke Zettlemoyer. 2018. Mapping language to code in programmatic context. *CoRR*, abs/1808.09588.

Taku Kudo and John Richardson. 2018. Sentencepiece: A simple and language independent subword tokenizer and detokenizer for neural text processing. *CoRR*, abs/1808.06226.

Marie-Anne Lachaux, Baptiste Roziere, Lowik Chanussot, and Guillaume Lample. 2020. Unsupervised translation of programming languages.

Jinhyuk Lee, Wonjin Yoon, Sungdong Kim, Donghyeon Kim, Sunkyu Kim, Chan Ho So, and Jaewoo Kang. 2019a. Biobert: a pre-trained biomedical language representation model for biomedical text mining. *CoRR*, abs/1901.08746.

Jinhyuk Lee, Wonjin Yoon, Sungdong Kim, Donghyeon Kim, Sunkyu Kim, Chan Ho So, and Jaewoo Kang. 2019b. Biobert: a pre-trained biomedical language representation model for biomedical text mining. *Bioinformatics*.

Mike Lewis, Yinhan Liu, Naman Goyal, Marjan Ghazvininejad, Abdelrahman Mohamed, Omer Levy, Veselin Stoyanov, and Luke Zettlemoyer. 2019. BART: denoising sequence-to-sequence pretraining for natural language generation, translation, and comprehension. *CoRR*, abs/1910.13461.

Yinhan Liu, Myle Ott, Naman Goyal, Jingfei Du, Mandar Joshi, Danqi Chen, Omer Levy, Mike Lewis, Luke Zettlemoyer, and Veselin Stoyanov. 2020. Ro{bert}a: A robustly optimized {bert} pretraining approach.

Shuai Lu, Daya Guo, Shuo Ren, Junjie Huang, Alexey Svyatkovskiy, Ambrosio Blanco, Colin Clement, Dawn Drain, Daxin Jiang, Duyu Tang, Ge Li, Lidong Zhou, Linjun Shou, Long Zhou, Michele Tufano, Ming Gong, Ming Zhou, Nan Duan, Neel Sundaresan, Shao Kun Deng, Shengyu Fu, and Shujie Liu. 2021. Codexglue: A machine learning benchmark dataset for code understanding and generation.

Kishore Papineni, Salim Roukos, Todd Ward, and Wei-Jing Zhu. 2002. Bleu: A method for automatic evaluation of machine translation. In *Proceedings of the 40th Annual Meeting on Association for Computational Linguistics*, ACL '02, page 311–318, USA. Association for Computational Linguistics.

Matthew E. Peters, Mark Neumann, Mohit Iyyer, Matt Gardner, Christopher Clark, Kenton Lee, and Luke Zettlemoyer. 2018. Deep contextualized word representations. *CoRR*, abs/1802.05365.

Colin Raffel, Noam Shazeer, Adam Roberts, Katherine Lee, Sharan Narang, Michael Matena, Yanqi Zhou, Wei Li, and Peter J. Liu. 2019. Exploring the limits of transfer learning with a unified text-to-text transformer. *CoRR*, abs/1910.10683.

Shuo Ren, Daya Guo, Shuai Lu, Long Zhou, Shujie Liu, Duyu Tang, Neel Sundaresan, Ming Zhou, Ambrosio Blanco, and Shuai Ma. 2020. Codebleu: a method for automatic evaluation of code synthesis.

Ashish Vaswani, Noam Shazeer, Niki Parmar, Jakob Uszkoreit, Llion Jones, Aidan N. Gomez, Lukasz Kaiser, and Illia Polosukhin. 2017. Attention is all you need. *CoRR*, abs/1706.03762.

Ronald J. Williams and David Zipser. 1989. A learning algorithm for continually running fully recurrent neural networks. *Neural Comput.*, 1(2):270–280.

Zhilin Yang, Zihang Dai, Yiming Yang, Jaime Carbonell, Ruslan Salakhutdinov, and Quoc V. Le. 2020. Xlnet: Generalized autoregressive pretraining for language understanding.

Pengcheng Yin, Graham Neubig, Wen tau Yih, and Sebastian Riedel. 2020. Tabert: Pretraining for joint understanding of textual and tabular data.

Yaqin Zhou, Shangqing Liu, Jingkai Siow, Xiaoning Du, and Yang Liu. 2019. Devign: Effective vulnerability identification by learning comprehensive program semantics via graph neural networks.

DIRECT : A Transformer-based Model for Decompiled Variable Name Recovery

Vikram Nitin * **Anthony Saieva** * **Baishakhi Ray** **Gail Kaiser**

Department of Computer Science, Columbia University

vikram.nitin@columbia.edu, {ant,rayb,kaiser}@cs.columbia.edu

Abstract

Decompiling binary executables to high-level code is an important step in reverse engineering scenarios, such as malware analysis and legacy code maintenance. However, the generated high-level code is difficult to understand since the original variable names are lost. In this paper, we leverage transformer models to reconstruct the original variable names from decompiled code. Inherent differences between code and natural language present certain challenges in applying conventional transformer-based architectures to variable name recovery. We propose DIRECT, a novel transformer-based architecture customized specifically for the task at hand. We evaluate our model on a dataset of decompiled functions and find that DIRECT outperforms the previous state-of-the-art model by up to 20%. We also present ablation studies evaluating the impact of each of our modifications. We make the source code of DIRECT available to encourage reproducible research.

1 Introduction

Proprietary software often comes in binary form, making it difficult to comprehend its functionality, as many high-level code abstractions (e.g., meaningful variable names, code structures, etc.) are lost when source code is compiled to binaries. To extract meaningful information from binaries, software analysts typically use reverse engineering that converts binary executables into another form that can be more easily comprehended (Ďurfina et al., 2013). Reverse engineering is often applied in binary code inspection, legacy software maintenance, malware analysis, and cyber forensics. For example, reverse engineering uncovered the rebirth of ZeUS malware variants during the coronavirus pandemic of 2020 (Osborne, 2020).

```
void __fastcall add_match(char *a1) {
  // ... var declarations omitted ...
  v1 = (int)(a1 - 1);
  while ( 1 ) {
    v3 = *(unsigned __int8 *)(v1++ + 1);
    v2 = v3;
    if ( !v3 ) break;
    v4 = v2 > 0x7F;
    if ( v2 != 127 )
      v4 = v2 > 0x1F;
    if ( !v4 ) {
      free(a1);
      return;
    }
  }
  // ... some code omitted ...
}
```

Figure 1: Real world Hex-Rays decompilation. Reconstructed source differs significantly from original, and it is hard to deduce original developers' intentions.

Traditionally, the primary reverse engineering tools are *disassemblers*, which extract assembly instructions from a binary executable. However, in recent years, *decompilers* like Ghidra (Ghidra) and Hex Rays (Hex-Rays) have become practical and popular. They produce a source code-like approximation of the binary code as shown in Figure 1. While these tools can retrieve the approximate code structure, they introduce variable names that have no semantic meaning, drastically reducing code readability and comprehensibility (Katz et al., 2018; Hu et al., 2018; Hayati et al., 2018).

In recent years, Machine Learning-based models have shown promise in recovering lost variable names from decompiled code using a frequency-based model (He et al., 2018) or LSTMs (Lacomis et al., 2019). However, variables in source code are not independent of each other and often have hidden long-range dependencies. LSTMs and frequency-based models are not well-suited to capture such dependencies. Since transformer-based models can more effectively capture long-range dependencies (Vaswani et al., 2017), in this work we explore transformer-based models to recover variable names from decompiled code.

* Equal contribution

Proceedings of the 1st Workshop on Natural Language Processing for Programming (NLP4Prog 2021), pages 48–57

Transformers are popular in natural language processing (Vaswani et al., 2017; Devlin et al., 2019; Yang et al., 2019). However, code differs from natural language in many significant ways (Allamanis et al., 2018; Ding et al., 2020), hence vanilla transformer architectures need modifications for practical application to the task of variable recovery. Consider the following problems:

Unknown number of tokens to be predicted: Transformers that capture bidirectional context usually predict a known number of tokens, but to make the vocabulary size manageable, identifiers must be split into subtokens. For example, an identifier like `my_var` could be split up as three subtokens - "`my`", "`_`", and "`var`". Each identifier can be comprised of an arbitrary number of subtokens, and the model needs to access the information contained in the entire sequence while predicting the name for an identifier. To deal with this problem, we use an encoder-decoder transformer architecture as in (Ahmad et al., 2021).

Syntactic constraints: Unlike natural language, code's strict syntax requires that a variable assigned a name at one occurrence in the prediction must be the same at all other occurrences. For example, if a decompiled identifier name `v1` appears on line 3 and line 100, the predicted name must be the same on both lines. We propose a novel algorithm that uses the joint probability over sequences to predict variable name identifiers while still obeying constraints imposed by the code syntax.

Token Non-uniformity: While training a model for natural language, all tokens are usually given equal importance (Vaswani et al., 2017). However, for semantic understanding of code the identifier tokens are more important than those tokens that are built into the language syntax. For example, a variable name like "`click_count`" provides much more sematic information than a keyword like "`while`". We propose a token weighting scheme specially crafted for the variable name recovery problem.

Code sequences are long: Adaptations of NLP techniques to code often consider functions analogous to sentences. Traditional transformers limit the maximum sequence size to a few hundred tokens. While this restriction rarely presents a problem dealing with sentences, many functions are much longer. For example, the longest function in our benchmark dataset (Section 4.1) is over 4000 tokens long. To handle longer functions we propose a mechanism to break long sequences into smaller pieces and recombine their individual predictions while still obeying code's syntactic constraints.

Putting all these together, we propose DIRECT (**D**ecompiled **I**dentifier **R**enaming **E**ngine using **C**ontextual **T**ransformers), the first transformer-based model built specially for variable recovery from decompiled binaries. We compare DIRECT to DIRE (Lacomis et al., 2019), the state of the art in variable name recovery on a benchmark dataset and show that DIRECT improves on the baseline by 20%. We also evaluate the individual impact of each of our specific adaptations by performing a series of ablation studies. We provide the source code for DIRECT [1] in the hope that it will prove to be a useful tool for other researchers.

2 Related Work

Variable Name Recovery: DIRE (Lacomis et al., 2019), compared to in the evaluation, performs the same task as DIRECT but uses traditional LSTMs combined with GGNNs. DIRECT uses DIRE's tokenizer as is, our innovations replace DIRE's bidirectional LSTM with our task-specific transformer architecture. Prior to DIRE, Debin (He et al., 2018) represented the prior state of the art using decision tree-based modeling.

Type Inference: Debin also attempted to recover type information – which is a different problem. Typilus (Allamanis et al., 2020) is a new GGNN-based approach for type inference.

Function Name Recovery: An orthogonal decompilation problem is function name recovery. Function names are usually left in executables' metadata, by default, but in malware these symbols are probably stripped. Recent work by Artuso et al. (Artuso et al., 2020) has shown transformers are highly applicable to this task and the pre-training/fine-tuning paradigm has a place in code analysis, but they limit their experiments to function names. Other work like David et al. (David et al., 2020) uses LSTM architectures to encode API call sequences as function profiles and learned the function names commonly associated with those call sequences.

Transformers for Filling-in Blanks: Filling in blanks in an input sequence necessitates a model that can capture bidirectional context. BERT's pre-training objective (Devlin et al., 2019) solves

[1] `https://github.com/DIRECT-team/DIRECT-nlp4prog`

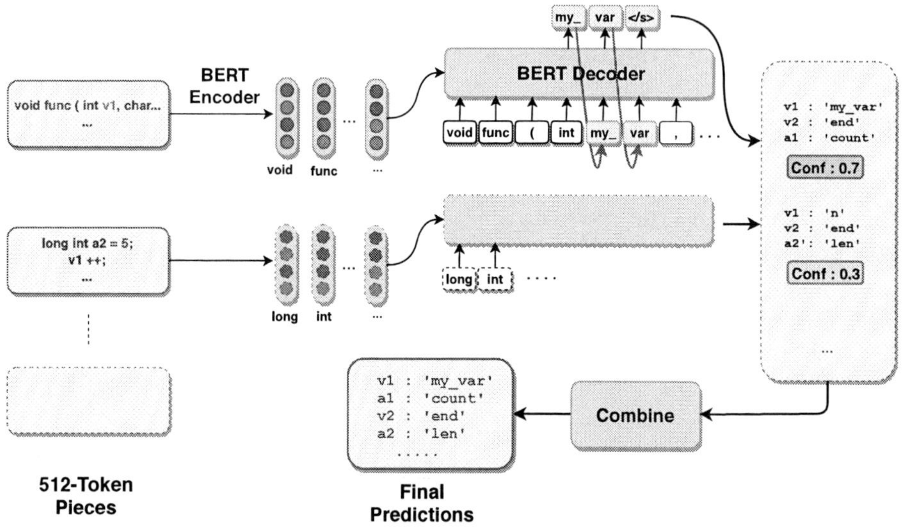

Figure 2: Our state-of-the-art variable renaming model, DIRECT. DIRECT breaks the function into pieces, passes each piece through a BERT encoder and decoder, and combines the predictions of all the pieces. For simplicity, we have omitted the advanced prediction algorithm (Algorithm 1; Figure 3) in this diagram. For more details, refer to Section 3.2.

this problem by reconstructing random masked tokens. SpanBERT (Joshi et al., 2020) focuses on contiguous spans of masked tokens with a modified pre-training objective. These methods require the location and length of each blank to be known in advance, but Insertion Transformers (Stern and Uszkoreit, 2019) solve for variable-length blanks without explicitly controlling insertion.

Blank Language Models (Shen et al., 2020) solve for fixed blanks with variable length with a special blank character that the model can predict and feed back in a loop. Another architecture that solves the same problem is BART (Lewis et al., 2020). Similar to us, BART uses a BERT encoder and a left-right decoder to perform arbitrary transformations on the input. However both these approaches cannot be directly applied to variable renaming without modification to guarantee that multiple blanks have the same prediction.

Decompilers: There are two decompilers used in practice. One is Hex-Rays (Hex-Rays), from which the training set was built, and the other is the open-source Ghidra platform (Ghidra), which both fail to make meaningful efforts at reconstructing variable names without debugging information. A research compiler DREAM++ (Yakdan et al., 2016) function signature heuristics to generate meaningful variable names, but does not apply ML models.

Adapting ML to SE tasks: Recent works like (Rahman et al., 2019) and (Ding et al., 2020) have also investigated the difficulties of applying ML models from other disciplines directly to software engineering tasks.

3 Design

Figure 2 provides an overview of DIRECT. In this section we detail each of the problems we encountered and the design decision solutions.

3.1 Encoding/Decoding

Transformers are traditionally used to predict entire sequences; however in our problem setting most tokens are fixed. Therefore we need to adapt transformers from predicting entire sequences to predicting individual tokens based on the fixed tokens.

While making a prediction on an occurrence of a particular variable, the model should ideally have access to the information contained in the entire input sequence. The naive solution is to use a bidirectional transformer that with a Masked Language Model (MLM) training scheme, such as BERT. However by design, an MLM is designed to predict the same number of tokens as in the input sequence. In our case, because of subtokenization, the predicted subsequences can be of unknown length. Adapting an MLM transformer to solve this problem is non-trivial.

The next option is to use a transformer as a

sequence-to-sequence language model to predict the immediate next token given all the preceding tokens. One could feed the entire sequence until a variable is reached, start generating tokens one at a time in an autoregressive manner, and stop when a special end token is predicted. However such a model cannot use bidirectional context while making a prediction, and can only leverage the part of the sequence that precedes each variable.

We propose to use an encoder-decoder setup, as in (Vaswani et al., 2017). The transformer encoder embeds each input token, and the sequential decoder attends over these encoder embeddings while making predictions one token at a time. So although we give the decoder only the portion of the input sequence that precedes the variable of interest, it also has access to the entire input sequence through the encoder embeddings.

Of course, this still leaves open the question of how to constrain multiple instances of the same variable to have the same prediction. While we will present a better solution to this problem in Section 3.2, a good first approximation is to simply use the prediction at the first occurrence of the variable we are interested in. We hypothesize that since the encoder-decoder model has access to the entire sentence while making a prediction for each occurrence, one cannot do drastically better than this simple approximation.

3.2 Advanced Prediction Algorithm

Effective sequence modeling requires not only making predictions, but also predictions that fit the problem setting (Ding et al., 2020). Semantic preserving identifier renaming mandates that once a variable has been renamed it must have the same value at each occurrence. This additional constraint poses a challenge for vanilla transformers since they predict each token independently in traditional language modeling. Exhaustively searching the target vocabulary space is computationally intractable, so we narrow the search space with a specialized prediction algorithm that fits the problem setting.

At the variable's first occurrence, we make m predictions for its name, each of which leads to a different sequence of variable name assignments. Throughout our algorithm, we maintain the top k sequences only. Thus at the first occurrence of a variable, we generate $m \times k$ possible sequences, and pick the top k. In practice, we use $m = k$.

At later occurrences of a variable, we update the scores of the existing predictions, thus maintaining the list of k sequences. This is where our algorithm differs from standard beam search. Note that the predictions made at the first occurrence of a variable constrain its predictions at further occurrences, but choosing a large k mitigates this problem.

This procedure, "Advanced prediction", is shown in Figure 3 for the case when $k = 2$. Algorithm 1 describes it in detail. In our experiments, we observed that choosing $k = 5$ was optimal.

Algorithm 1 Advanced Prediction

```
Input : A sequence of decompiler output tokens S, and a model M
Output : S with predicted names
gen ← [[ ]], probs ← [1]
for tok ∈ S do
    if tok is not a variable then
        for seq ∈ gen do
            seq.append(tok)
        continue
    if tok has been seen before then
        for j ∈ 1...len(gen) do
            n ← current pred of tok in gen[j]
            p ← prob assigned to n by M at the current position
            gen[j] ← gen[j] + p
            probs[j] ← probs[j] × p
    else
        for j ∈ 1...len(gen) do
            Using beam search over subtokens with M, find the top k possibilities for the name of tok
            Let the names be n_1, ..., n_k and their probabilities be p_1, ..., p_k
            Replace gen[j] with (gen[j] + n_1), ..., (gen[j] + n_k)
            Replace probs[j] with (probs[j] · p_1), ..., (probs[j] · p_k)
    Sort gen and probs in desc. order of probs
    gen ← gen[1 : k]
    probs ← probs[1 : k]
return gen[1]
```

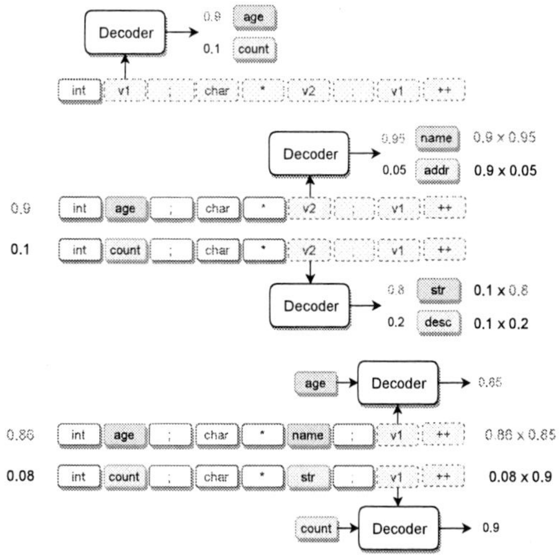

Figure 3: Advanced Prediction with $k = 2$. The decoder takes as input the portion of the sequence that *precedes* the variable being predicted. Our algorithm differs from standard beam search in the prediction of the second occurrence of `v1`. Rather than generate multiple predictions for `v1`, the algorithm simply updates the scores of the existing predictions in order to obey the syntactic constraints of code.

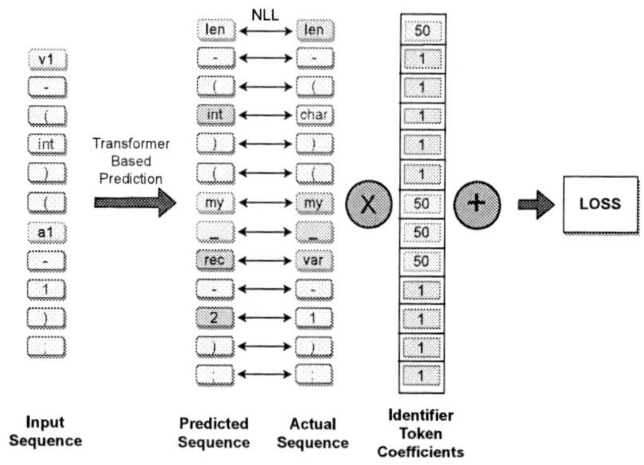

Figure 4: Identifier Token Coefficient loss function. The Negative Log Likelihood (NLL) loss is computed for each token, and a weighted sum taken to compute the loss.

3.3 Identifier Token Coefficient

A typical transformer treats all tokens identically when computing the loss function during pretraining and fine-tuning. Code differs from natural language in the grammar requires the majority of the tokens. The only opportunity for the programmer to inject semantic meaning into the source code text is through identifiers, which makes this problem compelling in the first place. The model should therefore treat identifier tokens differently.

We implement this concept by training with a custom loss function as shown in Figure 4. Traditional NLP architectures predict the entire sequence, and then train on a loss function by averaging the error uniformly across all tokens. Our custom weighting scheme places increased significance on prediction of identifiers, using a mask which increases the loss 50-fold for identifiers as compared to all other tokens. We expect that this *identifier token coefficient* (ITC) hyper parameter could be tuned in the future for better performance.

Predicting the identifiers and ignoring the rest of the characters in the sequence would result in a model that doesn't learn the context surrounding the identifier which informs the prediction.

3.4 Splitting and Merging Mechanism

Another inherent difference between code and natural language when considering sequence to sequence modeling is the length of the sequence. Discussion of natural language modeling overlooks this aspect since sentences rarely exceed 200 tokens. In code however functions are significantly longer so the ML models must support sequences of arbitrary length. In fact our benchmark dataset contains a small number of sequences with length greater than 2000. With respect to identifier recovery, longer sequences mean more variables to recover, multiple usages per variable, and more opportunity for errors. This poses a problem for transformers as traditional transformer based architectures, like BERT, require a maximum sequence length set in advance. Furthermore since attention must be trained across all tokens, the memory usage increases quadratically with sequence length.

In order to use our model for arbitrary sequence lengths, we developed a novel splitting and joint prediction mechanism. As described in Figure 2 we divide the sequence into multiple chunks of 512 tokens upon which the model predicts. A single variable can have a different prediction in each chunk we combine these predictions using the prediction at the first chunk in which a variable occurs.

We also tried using the chunk with the highest confidence, but we found that this did not perform as well. We suspect this is because the probabilities are less than one, and multiplications with each successive variable only decrease the probability of the entire sequence. Hence smaller pieces with perhaps just one or two occurrences of a variable will be more confident in their predictions despite having less information. One could impose a penalty for pieces with fewer variables, but we defer this analysis to future work.

Other transformer variants can handle sequences arbitrary lengths like XLNet (Yang et al., 2019), and we expect these advanced models will handle this issue as well as present new challenges. We again leave these endeavors to future work.

3.5 DIRECT

Using the techniques from the previous sections, we put it all together to get DIRECT, a state-of-the-art variable renaming system. Given an input sequence, DIRECT splits it into pieces of length at most 512 each (default BERT architecture), and puts each piece through a BERT encoder and a BERT decoder with advanced prediction (Algorithm 1). Different predictions across pieces for the same variable are combined by taking the prediction of the first piece in the sequence that contains the variable. Figure 2 depicts the entire model.

4 Experimental Setup

4.1 Data

We use the dataset provided by DIRE (Lacomis et al., 2019). It was generated using C binaries from Github, which were then decompiled using Ida's Hex-Rays decompilation plugin (Hex-Rays). The training data set consists of 1,011,049 functions, with a median of 16 variables per function, a median of 4 *unique* variables per function, and a median sequence length of 150 subtokens. We follow DIRE and use Sentencepiece (Kudo and Richardson, 2018) to split the functions into subtokens.

We use only the "Body-not-in-train" subset for the validation and test data. They consist of 23662 and 24862 examples, respectively.

4.2 Metrics

We define *accuracy* as an exact match between the original variable name as determined by the debug information mapping, and the name predicted by DIRECT. We also examine the *edit distance* between predicted names and true names, and use the edit distance per number of characters (the character error rate) as our metric as in DIRE (Lacomis et al., 2019) to capture success of partial matches. We also measure the *Jaccard similarity* which is the ratio of the number of overlapping n-grams between two sequences to the total number of n-grams contained in them. We use n=1, so that each word is treated as a set of its constituent characters. There are some instances when decompiler variables have no corresponding true name. These are ignored from all metrics.

4.3 Pre-training Procedure

We pre-train one BERT model using the standard MLM task on source sequences directly from the decompiler output (with the dummy variable names from the decompiler). We call this the BERT encoder. Similarly we pre-train another BERT model using MLM on target sentences (with the true variable names), and call this the BERT decoder. Both models used 4 attention heads, 6 hidden layers, and a hidden embedding size of 256. We trained the encoder and decoder for 220k and 140k steps, respectively, using a batch size of 128 sequences. While masking tokens, we do not differentiate between variable and non-variable tokens since we want the model to learn the complete structure of the code sequences. We also used the standard optimization techniques employed by BERT (Devlin et al., 2019), wherein an Adam optimizer is used with a variable learning rate. The learning rate increases linearly from 0 to 10^{-4} over the "warm-up" period of 40k iterations, and then decreases linearly from 10^{-4} to 0 at the end of pre-training.

4.4 Fine-tuning Procedure

After reviewing our proof of concept experiments we trained our best configuration for 85 epochs to produce the DIRECT prototype. We follow the same convention as DIRE (Lacomis et al., 2019), whereby the number of sequences per batch is variable, but the total number of tokens in the batch is fixed to define the size of the batch. We used a batch size of 4096 tokens per batch. We used a learning rate of 1e-4 for the first 10 epochs, 0.3e-4 for the next 10, and 1e-5 thereafter.

5 Results

5.1 DIRECT Evaluation

In order to evaluate the effectiveness of DIRECT, we compare its performance against that of DIRE on our test dataset. The results are shown in Table 1. We observe that DIRECT achieves an increase of 7.1 percentage points in accuracy over DIRE, which is a relative increase of 19.9%. We obtained all DIRE results by re-running the authors' code on

Model	Accuracy (%) ↑	Top-5 Accuracy (%) ↑	CER ↓	Jaccard Dist ↓
DIRE	35.8	41.5	.664	.537
DIRECT	**42.8**	**49.3**	**.663**	**.501**
Improvement	20%	19%	.2%	6.5%

Table 1: Test Accuracy, Top-5 Accuracy (computed by taking the top 5 predictions for each *sequence* and using the predictions of variables contained in these sequences), Character Error Rate and Jaccard distance of DIRE vs DIRECT. DIRECT outperforms DIRE on all four metrics. DIRE results are reproduced by re-running the authors' code on our dataset.

```
signed __int64 __fastcall prussdrv_open ( unsigned int
host_interrupt ) {
    char name ;
    unsigned __int64 @@v3@@ ;
    @@v3@@ = __readfsqword ( Number ) ;
    if ( dword_15A4 [ @@v1@@ ] ) return Number ;
    sprintf ( & name , String , @@v1@@ ) ;
    dword_15A4 [ @@v1@@ ] = open ( & name , Number ) ;
    return _prussdrv_memmap_init ( ) ;
    }
```

```
signed __int64 __fastcall prussdrv_open ( unsigned int
host_interrupt ) {
    char name ;
    unsigned __int64 @@v3@@ ;
    @@v3@@ = __readfsqword ( Number ) ;
    if ( dword_15A4 [ host_interrupt ] ) return Number ;
    sprintf ( & name , String , host_interrupt ) ;
    dword_15A4 [ host_interrupt ] = open ( & name ,
  Number ) ;
    return _prussdrv_memmap_init ( ) ;
```

Figure 5: A visualization of the attention weights of the trained decoder while predicting variables. Darker represents larger weights. The variable subtokens that are being predicted are boxed. For more details, refer to Section 5.

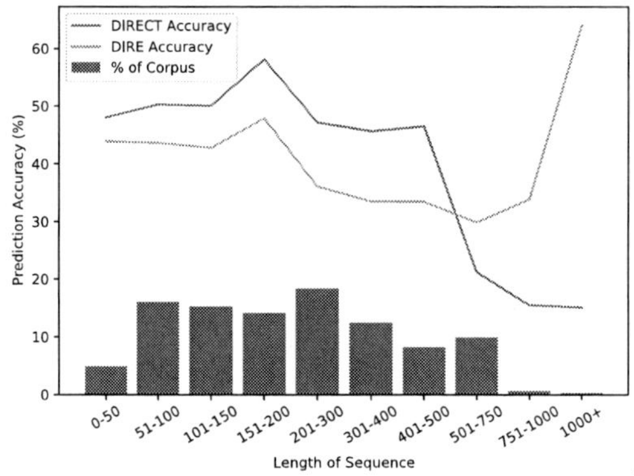

Figure 6: Variation of Accuracy of DIRECT and DIRE with length. The spike in DIRE's performance for the last two categories with very few examples is likely to be an anomaly and not representative of its true performance on sequences of those lengths. Note that this is on the validation set.

the dataset, rather than simply using the numbers from their paper.

5.2 Qualitative Analysis

We also perform some qualitative inspection of the attention weights of the trained model to understand what information it is using to make its inferences. An example of this is shown in Figure 5 where the predicted identifier is outlined in black. The attentions shown are the weights used while predicting a name for the variable shown in a box, averaged over all attention heads at the last layer of the decoder.

We observe that when making a prediction on the first occurrence of a variable, the decoder model pays attention mainly to the function header, more specifically the return type and function name. However for later occurrences of the same variable, although it does look at the function header to some extent, it relies chiefly on its predictions for earlier instances of the same variable.

5.3 Performance on Long Sequences

The graph in Figure 6 shows the accuracy of DIRECT on sequences of various lengths. As we cross the 500 token mark, and the splitting technique takes over, there is a steep drop in accuracy. This problem is mirrored in DIRE's accuracy although not quite as steeply. Still for sequences of length less than 512 tokens DIRECT has a improvement of 10 percentage points over DIRE (48.9% vs. 38.8%). DIRE has high accuracy in the longest two sets of sequences, but this is likely an anomaly caused by insufficient samples sizes.

Other transformer based variants address this sequence issue such as XLNet (Yang et al., 2019), and we expect these advanced models will handle this issue as well as present new challenges. We again leave these endeavors to future work.

Model	Accuracy (%) ↑	CER ↓
Uniform token weighting	30.0	.80
Weighting identifiers only	33.7	.76
ITC weighting scheme	**34.4**	**.75**

Table 2: Validation accuracy and Character Error Rate for various token weighting schemes. Prediction is done using the "first prediction" strategy. All the models are trained for 15 epochs. Refer to Section 3.3 for more details.

Model	Accuracy (%) ↑	CER ↓
First pred	34.4	**.75**
Advanced pred	**34.6**	**.75**

Table 3: Validation accuracy and Character Error Rate for advanced prediction versus first prediction. Both models are trained for 15 epochs. Refer to Section 3.2 for more details.

Model	Accuracy (%)	CER
Decoder Only	19.6	.97
Encoder-Decoder	**34.4**	**.75**

Table 4: Validation accuracy and Character Error Rate for our encoder-decoder model versus a decoder-only model. Both models are trained for 15 epochs. Refer to Section 3.1 for more details.

5.4 Ablation Studies

In this section, we evaluate the impact of each of our design choices. We train all the models for 15 epochs and evaluate them on the *validation* set.

5.4.1 Encoder-Decoder Architecture

Table 4 shows the performance of our encoder-decoder model vs a decoder-only model (a single transformer, operating as an autoregressive language model) using the prediction at the *first* occurrence of each variable. As we can see, the decoder-only model does significantly worse, which is expected since it has access only to a part of the function while making a prediction at the first instance of a variable.

5.4.2 Advanced Prediction Algorithm

Table 3 compares the results of advanced prediction with "first prediction", i.e., taking the prediction at the first occurrence of a variable. We observe that advanced prediction improves the performance of our encoder-decoder model by a small amount.

This could be explained by our observation in Section 5.2 that the model seems to rely its earlier predictions while predicting the name of a particular variable. Later predictions of a variable refer to the value assigned at the first prediction, and so the prediction of a variable seldom changes from what was predicted at the first instance.

5.4.3 Identifier Token Coefficient

We compare the performance of three different token weighting schemes in the loss function - weighting all tokens uniformly, weighting according to ITC (as described in Section 3.3), and weighting the identifiers only while ignoring the rest of the tokens.

As seen in Table 2, ITC shows a 4.4% increase in accuracy relative to the uniform weighting scheme, *without* hyperparameter tuning of the coefficient. As expected the model that ignores the surrounding tokens in the loss function performs worse. This is because the model doesn't effectively learn the context surrounding the identifiers, resulting in a decrease in accuracy by 0.7 percentage points.

6 Conclusion and Future Work

The problem of variable name reconstruction poses certain challenges for traditional transformer-based models. Specifically, the variable length of the prediction target, the constraints imposed by code syntax, architecture limitations that make long sequences difficult, and the task specific non-uniformity of token significance. In this work, we developed a series of solutions to address these issues, namely 1) an encoding/decoding scheme to handle arbitrary sub-token length prediction, 2) a specialized prediction algorithm, 3) a customized identifier token coefficient weighting scheme, and 4) a splitting and combining algorithm for standard transformers to handle sequences of arbitrary length. In addition to empirical studies evaluating the effectiveness of each of these techniques, we also combined them to create DIRECT, a practical open-sourced identifier renaming engine. We evaluated DIRECT using a standard benchmark dataset against the state of the art, DIRE (Lacomis et al., 2019), and found that DIRECT provides a 20% improvement. We hope that in addition to an open-sourced tool, this work functions as a roadmap for other researchers trying to solve the types of problems we encountered when adapting transformer-based models to code analysis tasks. Future work could leverage the Abstract Syntax Tree (AST) of each function, and employ new transformer architectures like XLNet (Yang et al., 2019) to avoid splitting up the input while handling longer sequences. Our approach might also improve the results of other code analysis tasks like type inference, function re-naming, docstring prediction, and function boundary identification.

7 Acknowledgements

This work was supported in part by DARPA N6600121C4018, NSF CCF-1815494, NSF CNS-1563555, NSF CCF-1845893, NSF CCF-1822965, NSF CNS-1842456. We thank the anonymous reviewers for their helpful feedback. We would also like to thank Suman Jana for his generous provision of computing resources.

References

Wasi Uddin Ahmad, Saikat Chakraborty, Baishakhi Ray, and Kai-Wei Chang. 2021. Unified pre-training for program understanding and generation. *arXiv preprint arXiv:2103.06333*.

Miltiadis Allamanis, Earl T Barr, Premkumar Devanbu, and Charles Sutton. 2018. A survey of machine learning for big code and naturalness. *ACM Computing Surveys (CSUR)*, 51(4):1–37.

Miltiadis Allamanis, Earl T Barr, Soline Ducousso, and Zheng Gao. 2020. Typilus: Neural Type Hints. In *41st ACM SIGPLAN Conference on Programming Language Design and Implementation (PLDI)*, pages 91–105.

Fiorella Artuso, Giuseppe Antonio Di Luna, Luca Massarelli, and Leonardo Querzoni. 2020. In Nomine Function: Naming Functions in Stripped Binaries with Neural Networks. *arXiv preprint arXiv:1912.07946*.

Yaniv David, Uri Alon, and Eran Yahav. 2020. Neural Reverse Engineering of Stripped Binaries. *arXiv preprint arXiv:1902.09122*.

Jacob Devlin, Ming-Wei Chang, Kenton Lee, and Kristina Toutanova. 2019. BERT: Pre-training of Deep Bidirectional Transformers for Language Understanding. In *17th Annual Conference of the North American Chapter of the Association for Computational Linguistics: Human Language Technologies (NAACL-HLT)*, pages 4171–4186.

Yangruibo Ding, Baishakhi Ray, Premkumar Devanbu, and Vincent J Hellendoorn. 2020. Patching as translation: the data and the metaphor. In *2020 35th IEEE/ACM International Conference on Automated Software Engineering (ASE)*, pages 275–286. IEEE.

Ghidra. 2021. GHIDRA, A software reverse engineering (SRE) suite of tools developed by NSA's Research Directorate in support of the Cybersecurity mission. `https://ghidra-sre.org/`.

Shirley Anugrah Hayati, Raphael Olivier, Pravalika Avvaru, Pengcheng Yin, Anthony Tomasic, and Graham Neubig. 2018. Retrieval-based neural code generation. *Proceedings of the 2018 Conference on Empirical Methods in Natural Language Processing*.

Jingxuan He, Pesho Ivanov, Petar Tsankov, Veselin Raychev, and Martin Vechev. 2018. Debin: Predicting Debug Information in Stripped Binaries. In *ACM SIGSAC Conference on Computer and Communications Security*, pages 1667–1680.

Hex-Rays. 2021. Hex-Rays Decompiler. `https://hex-rays.com/decompiler/`.

Xing Hu, Ge Li, Xin Xia, David Lo, and Zhi Jin. 2018. Deep code comment generation. In *2018 IEEE/ACM 26th International Conference on Program Comprehension (ICPC)*, pages 200–20010. IEEE.

Mandar Joshi, Danqi Chen, Yinhan Liu, Daniel S. Weld, Luke Zettlemoyer, and Omer Levy. 2020. Spanbert: Improving pre-training by representing and predicting spans. *Transactions of the Association for Computational Linguistics*, 8:64–77.

Deborah S Katz, Jason Ruchti, and Eric Schulte. 2018. Using recurrent neural networks for decompilation. In *2018 IEEE 25th International Conference on Software Analysis, Evolution and Reengineering (SANER)*, pages 346–356. IEEE.

Taku Kudo and John Richardson. 2018. Sentencepiece: A simple and language independent subword tokenizer and detokenizer for neural text processing. *arXiv preprint arXiv:1808.06226*.

Jeremy Lacomis, Pengcheng Yin, Edward J. Schwartz, Miltiadis Allamanis, Claire Le Goues, Graham Neubig, and Bogdan Vasilescu. 2019. DIRE: A Neural Approach to Decompiled Identifier Naming. In *34th IEEE/ACM International Conference on Automated Software Engineering (ASE)*, pages 628—-639.

Mike Lewis, Yinhan Liu, Naman Goyal, Marjan Ghazvininejad, Abdelrahman Mohamed, Omer Levy, Veselin Stoyanov, and Luke Zettlemoyer. 2020. Bart: Denoising sequence-to-sequence pre-training for natural language generation, translation, and comprehension. *Proceedings of the 58th Annual Meeting of the Association for Computational Linguistics*.

Charlie Osborne. 2020. Zeus sphinx revamped as coronavirus relief payment attack wave continues. `https://tinyurl.com/ka2t6k2r`.

Md Masudur Rahman, Saikat Chakraborty, Gail Kaiser, and Baishakhi Ray. 2019. Toward Optimal Selection of Information Retrieval Models for Software Engineering Tasks. In *19th International Working Conference on Source Code Analysis and Manipulation (SCAM)*, pages 127–138.

Tianxiao Shen, Victor Quach, Regina Barzilay, and Tommi Jaakkola. 2020. Blank Language Models. *arXiv preprint arXiv:2002.03079*.

Kiros Stern, Chan and Uszkoreit. 2019. Insertion transformer: Flexible sequence generation via insertion operations. `https://arxiv.org/abs/1902.03249`.

Ashish Vaswani, Noam Shazeer, Niki Parmar, Jakob Uszkoreit, Llion Jones, Aidan N. Gomez, Lukasz Kaiser, and Illia Polosukhin. 2017. Attention Is All You Need. In *31st Conference on Neural Information Processing Systems (NIPS)*.

Khaled Yakdan, Sergej Dechand, Elmar Gerhards-Padilla, and Matthew Smith. 2016. Helping Johnny to Analyze Malware: A Usability-Optimized Decompiler and Malware Analysis User Study. In *IEEE Symposium on Security and Privacy (S&P)*, pages 158–177.

Zhilin Yang, Zihang Dai, Yiming Yang, Jaime Carbonell, Ruslan Salakhutdinov, and Quoc V. Le. 2019. XLNet: Generalized Autoregressive Pretraining for Language Understanding. In *33rd Conference on Neural Information Processing Systems (NIPS)*.

Lukás Ďurfina, Jakub Křoustek, and Petr Zemek. 2013. Psybot malware: A step-by-step decompilation case study. In *2013 20th Working Conference on Reverse Engineering (WCRE)*, pages 449–456.

Shellcode_IA32: A Dataset for Automatic Shellcode Generation

Pietro Liguori[1], **Erfan Al-Hossami**[2], **Domenico Cotroneo**[1], **Roberto Natella**[1], **Bojan Cukic**[2] and **Samira Shaikh**[2]

[1]University of Naples Federico II , Naples, Italy
[2]University of North Carolina at Charlotte, Charlotte, NC, USA
{pietro.liguori, cotroneo, roberto.natella}@unina.it
{ealhossa, bcukic, samirashaikh}@uncc.edu

Abstract

We take the first step to address the task of automatically generating shellcodes, i.e., small pieces of code used as a payload in the exploitation of a software vulnerability, starting from natural language comments. We assemble and release a novel dataset (*Shellcode_IA32*), consisting of challenging but common assembly instructions with their natural language descriptions. We experiment with standard methods in neural machine translation (NMT) to establish baseline performance levels on this task.

```
1  global _start;      Declare global _start.
2  section .text;      Declare the text section.

3  _start:;            Define the _start label.
4  xor eax, eax;       Zero out the eax
                       register
5  push eax;           and push its contents
                       on the stack.
6  push 0x68732f2f;Move /bin//sh
7  push 0x6e69622f;into the ebx register.
8  mov ebx, esp
9  push eax;           Push the contents of eax
                       onto the stack
10 mov edx, esp;       and point edx to the
                       stack register.
11 push ebx;           Push the contents of ebx
                       onto the stack
12 mov ecx, esp;       and point ecx to the
                       stack register.
13 mov al, 11;         Put the system call 11
                       into the al register.
14 int 0x80;           Make the kernel call.
```

Listing 1: x86 assembly code used to spawn /bin/sh shell on Linux OS. Lines 4-5, 6-7-8, 9-10, 11-12 are multi-line snippets generated by four different intents.

1 Introduction and Related Work

A growing body of research has dealt with automated code generation: given a natural language description, a code comment or intent, the task is to generate a piece of code in a programming language (Yin and Neubig, 2017; Ling et al., 2016). The task of generating programming code snippets, also referred to as semantic parsing (Yin and Neubig, 2019; Xu et al., 2020), has been previously addressed to generate executable snippets in domain-specific languages (Guu et al., 2017; Long et al., 2016), and several programming languages, including Python (Yin and Neubig, 2017) and Java (Ling et al., 2016).

We consider the task of generating *shellcodes*, i.e., small pieces of code used as a payload to exploit software vulnerabilities. Shellcoding, in its most literal sense, means writing code that will return a remote shell when executed. It can represent any byte code that will be inserted into an exploit to accomplish the desired, malicious, task (Mason et al., 2009). An example of a shellcode program in assembly language and the corresponding natural language comments are shown in Listing 1.

Shellcodes are important because they are the key element of security attacks: they represent code injected into victim software to take control of a machine, to escalate privileges, and to use the machine for malicious purposes such as DDoS attacks, data theft, and running malware (Arce, 2004). Well-intentioned actors (security practitioners and product vendors) also develop shellcodes to run non-harmful *proof-of-concept* attacks, to show how security weaknesses can be exploited to identify vulnerabilities and patch systems. Thus, shellcode generation using (semi-) automated techniques has become a popular and very active research topic (Bao et al., 2017). However, writing shellcodes is technically challenging since they are typically written in assembly language (c.f. Listing 1). The most sophisticated shellcodes can reach hundreds of assembly lines of code.

The task of the shellcode generation has been addressed by several works and tools. Bao *et al.* (2017) designed ShellSwap, a system that can modify an observed exploit and replace the original

Proceedings of the 1st Workshop on Natural Language Processing for Programming (NLP4Prog 2021), pages 58–64
August 1–6, 2021. ©2021 Association for Computational Linguistics

shellcode with an arbitrary replacement shellcode. The system uses symbolic tracing, with a combination of shellcode layout remediation and path kneading to achieve shellcode transplants. *Pwntools* (pwntools, Accessed: 2021-05-29) is a CTF framework and exploit development library written in Python. It is designed for rapid prototyping and development and intended to make exploit writing as simple as possible.

Differently from previous work in the security literature, we approach this problem as a machine translation (NMT) task. We apply neural machine translation (Goodfellow et al., 2016), which unlike the traditional phrase-based translation system consisting of many small sub-components tuned separately, attempts to build and train a single, large neural network that reads a sentence and outputs a correct translation (Bahdanau et al., 2015). NMT has emerged as a promising machine translation approach, showing superior performance on public benchmarks (Bojar et al., 2016), and it is widely recognized as the premier method for the translation of different languages (Wu et al., 2016). NMT has also been used to perform complex tasks on the UNIX operating system shell (Lin et al., 2017) (e.g. file manipulation and search), by stating goals in English (Lin et al., 2018), to automatically generate commit messages (Liu et al., 2018), etc. However, the NMT techniques have not heretofore been adopted to automatically generate software exploits from natural language comments.

Since NMT is a data-driven approach to code generation, we need a dataset of intents in natural language, and their corresponding translation (in our context, in assembly language) for shellcode generation. In this preliminary work, we address the lack of such a dataset by presenting *Shellcode_IA32*, a dataset containing 3, 200 lines of assembly code extracted from real shellcodes and described in the English language. Moreover, we present experiments on our dataset using a baseline technique, in order to establish performance levels for evaluating shellcode generation techniques.

2 Dataset

We compiled a dataset, ***Shellcode_IA32***, specific to our task. This dataset consists of 3,200 examples of instructions in assembly language for *IA-32* (the 32-bit version of the x86 Intel Architecture) from publicly-available security exploits. We collected assembly programs used to generate shellcode from *shell-storm* (Shellcodes database for study cases, Accessed: 2021-04-22) and from *Exploit Database* (Exploit Database Shellcodes , Accessed: 2021-04-22), in the period between 2000 and 2020.

Our focus is on Linux, the most common OS for security-critical network services. Accordingly, we added assembly instructions written with *Netwide Assembler* (NASM) for Linux (Duntemann, 2000). NASM is line-based. Figure 1 shows a simple example of a NASM source line. Every source line contains a combination of four fields: an optional *label* used to represent either an identifier or a constant, a *mnemonic* or *instruction*, which identifies the purpose of the statement and followed by zero or more *operands* specifying the data to be manipulated, and an optional *comment*, i.e., text ignored by the compiler. A mnemonic is not required if a line contains only a label or a comment.

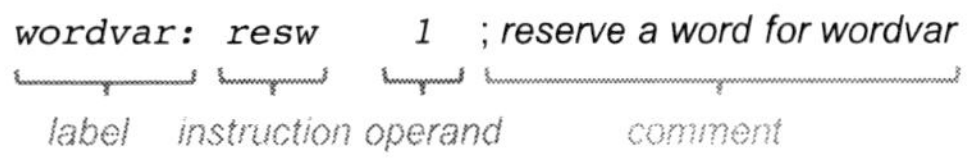

Figure 1: Layout of NASM source line

Each line of *Shellcode_IA32* dataset represents a snippet – intent pair. The **snippet** is a line or a combination of multiple lines of assembly code, built by following the NASM syntax. The **intent** is a comment in the English language (c.f. Listing 1).

To take into account the variability of descriptions in natural language, multiple authors described independently different samples of the dataset in the English language. Where available, we used as natural language descriptions the comments written by developers of the collected programs. We enriched the dataset by adding examples of assembly programs for the IA-32 architecture from popular tutorials and books (Duntemann, 2011; Kusswurm, 2014; Tutorialspoint, Accessed: 2021-04-22) to understand how different authors and assembly experts describe the code and, thus, how to deal with the ambiguity of natural language in this specific context. Our dataset consists of $\sim 10\%$ of instructions collected from books and guidelines and the rest from real shellcodes.

Multi-line Snippets: To automatically generate shellcodes, we need to look beyond a one-to-one mapping between a line of code and its comment/intent. For example, a common operation in shellcodes is to save the ASCII *"/bin/sh"* into a register. This operation requires three distinct assembly

Intent: *jump short to the decode label if the contents of the* `al` *register is not equal to the contents of the* `cl` *register else jump to the shellcode label*
Multi-line Snippets: `cmp al, cl \n jne short decode \n jmp shellcode`

Intent: *jump to the label recv_http_request if the contents of the* `eax` *register is not zero else subtract the value* `0x6` *from the contents of the* `ecx` *register*
Multi-line Snippets: `test eax, eax \n jnz recv_http_request \n sub ecx, 0x6`

Table 1: Examples of multi-line snippets

Statistics	Natural Language	Assembly Language
Unique Statements	3,184	2,248
Unique Tokens	1,498	1,244
Avg. tokens per statement	9.22	4.38
Min tokens per statement	1	2
Max tokens per statement	46	30

Table 2: *Shellcode_IA32* statistics

instructions: push the hexadecimal values of the words *"/bin"* and *"//sh"* onto the stack register before moving the contents of the stack register into the destination register (lines 6-8 in Listing 1). It would be meaningless to consider these three instructions as separate. To address such situations, we include 510 lines ($\sim$ 16% of the dataset) of intents that generate multiple lines of shellcodes (separated by the newline character \n). Table 1 shows two further examples of multi-line snippets with their natural language intent.

Statistics: Table 2 presents the descriptive statistics of the *Shellcode_IA32* dataset. The dataset contains 52 distinct assembly instructions (excluding function, section, and label declaration). The two most frequent assembly instructions are `mov` ($\sim$ 30% frequency), used to move data into/from registers/memory or to invoke a system call, and `push` ($\sim$ 22% frequency), which is used to push a value onto the stack. The next most frequent instructions are the `cmp` ($\sim$ 7% frequency), `xor` and `jmp` instructions ($\sim$ 4% frequency). The *low-frequency words* (i.e., the words that appear only once or twice in the dataset) contribute to the 3.6% and 7.3% of the natural language and the assembly language, resp. Figure 2 shows the distribution of the number of tokens across the intents and snippets in the dataset. We publicly share our entire *Shellcode_IA32* dataset on a GitHub repository.[1]

Size of our dataset: Our dataset contains 3,200 instances, which may seem relatively small compared to training data available for most common NLP tasks. We note, however, that our dataset is comparable in size to the CoNaLa annotated dataset (2,379 training and 500 test examples), which is one of the standard datasets in code generation (for English-Python code generation) (Yin et al., 2018). Further, *Shellcode_IA32* contains a higher percentage of multi-line snippets ($\sim$ 16% vs. $\sim$ 4%). We also note here that existing code generation datasets do contain a larger, potentially noisy, subset of training examples (ranging in several thousand) obtained by mining the web. For example, the CoNaLa *mined* (as opposed to the CoNaLa *annotated*) dataset contains 598,237 training examples mined directly from Stack Overflow (Yin et al., 2018). In our case, although shellcodes are written in assembly language, it is not feasible to simply mine examples of natural language–assembly from the web: not all assembly programs are shellcodes. Thus, our *Shellcode_IA32* dataset, which contains $\sim$ 20 years of shellcodes from a variety of sources is the largest collection of shellcodes in assembly available to date.

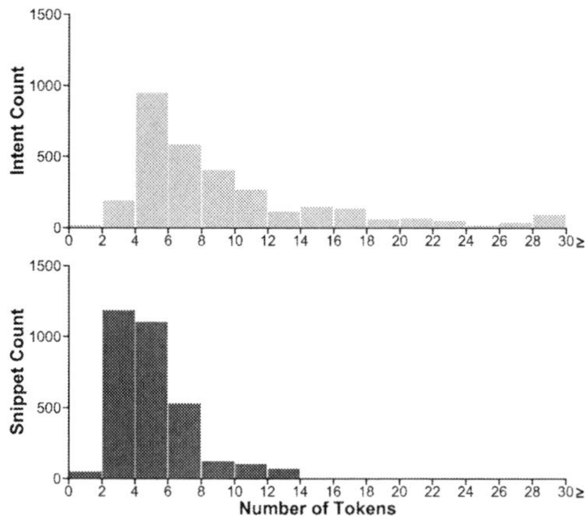

Figure 2: Histogram of the *Shellcode_IA32* dataset showcasing the distribution of token counts across intents and snippets.

3 Preliminary Evaluation

We performed a set of preliminary experiments with our dataset, in order to assess the applicability

[1]The dataset can be found here: `https://github.com/dessertlab/Shellcode_IA32`

Number Layers	Layer Dimension	BLEU-1 (%)	BLEU-2 (%)	BLEU-3 (%)	BLEU-4 (%)	ACC (%)
1	64	75.75	69.76	65.14	60.8	34.69
	128	80.80	76.29	73.10	69.69	42.5
	256	75.50	70.50	66.65	62.86	43.75
	512	**83.55**	**80.08**	**78.06**	**76.12**	**51.25**
2	64	63.25	53.24	46.12	39.46	15.62
	128	71.79	64.24	58.25	51.65	26.25
	256	75.13	68.63	63.94	58.93	25.62
	512	**80.22**	**75.00**	**71.11**	**67.24**	**43.44**
3	64	61.98	50.68	43.02	36.15	9.38
	128	69.75	61.08	55.09	49.18	19.06
	256	**76.93**	**71.32**	**67.41**	**63.50**	**31.87**
	512	74.99	68.58	64.23	60.36	29.38
4	64	61.41	50.68	43.58	37.33	10.00
	128	63.26	51.98	44.62	37.57	10.94
	256	66.94	57.85	51.97	46.87	15.31
	512	**70.51**	**62.44**	**56.27**	**50.15**	**18.75**

Table 3: Performance results obtained by varying the model hyper-parameters. The best performances for each number of layers are in bold.

of NMT in the context of shellcode generation and to establish baseline performance levels for evaluating techniques for future research. Similar to the encoder-decoder architecture with attention (Bahdanau et al., 2015), we use a bi-directional LSTM as the encoder to transform an embedded intent sequence $E = |e_1, ..., e_{T_S}|$ into a vector c of hidden states with equal length. We implement this architecture with Bahdanau-style attention (Bahdanau et al., 2015) using `xnmt` (Neubig et al., 2018). We use an Adam optimizer (Kingma and Ba, 2015) with $\beta_1 = 0.9$ and $\beta_2 = 0.999$. The last step is inference. During inference, the auto regressive inference component uses beam search with a beam size of 5. The train/dev/test split is train (N = 2560), dev (N = 320), and test (N = 320) using a random $80/10/10$ ratio. The test set includes 44 multi-line snippets (13.75% of the test set).

Following prior work in this area (Ling et al., 2016; Yin and Neubig, 2017; Oda et al., 2015), we evaluate the translation performance in terms of averaged token level BLEU scores (Papineni et al., 2002). BLEU uses the modified form of n-grams precision and length difference penalty to evaluate the quality of the output generated by the model compared to the referenced one. BLEU measures translation quality by the accuracy of translating ngrams to n-grams, for values of n usually ranging between 1 and 4 (Han, 2016; Munkova et al., 2020). We measure the performance of the evaluation task also in terms of exact match accuracy (ACC), which is the fraction of exactly matching samples between the predicted output and the reference (Yin and Neubig, 2017). Both metrics range between 0 and 1.

During our experiments, we set a basic configuration of the model: $\alpha = 0.001$, layers = 1, vocabulary size = $4,000$, epochs (with early stopping enforced) = 200, beam size = 5, *minimun word frequency* = 1. Next, we performed experiments by varying the dimensionality of the layers from 64 to 1024, and the number of layers from 1 to 4 while keeping all other hyper-parameters constant. Table 3 summarizes the results. We notice that increasing the number of layers leads to worse performance, while a layer dimension set between 256 and 512 is found to be the best option.

All experiments were performed on a Linux OS running on a virtual machine with 8 CPU cores and 8 GB RAM. The computational times are highly dependent on the model hyper-parameters, and range between few minutes to $\sim$ 105 minutes, with the average training time equal to $\sim$ 28 minutes.

4 Qualitative Analysis

Automated metrics (BLEU and accuracy) provide a somewhat limited window into the efficacy of the models to accomplish our task: the task of automatically generating assembly code from natural language intents. We conducted a qualitative analysis of the outputs to address this issue and present our findings through cherry- and lemon picked examples from our test set (Table 4). In particular, we manually expected the outputs predicted by the

Natural Language	Ground Truth	Model Output

Put ASCII /bin/sh into eax	`push 0x68732f2f \n`
	`push 0x6e69622f \n`
	`mov eax , esp`
		`push 0x68732f2f \n`
		`push 0x6e69622f \n`
		`mov eax, esp`

Place address buff into esi	`mov esi, buff`	`lea esi, [buff]`
Perform a bit-wise inversion of edx	`not edx`	**`and edx, 0`**
if the contents of the bl register is greater than or equal to the value 78h then jump to the memory location loc_402B1D	`cmp bl, 78h \n jge short loc_402B1D`	`cmp bl, 78h \n` **`jle`** `short loc_402B1D`

Table 4: Illustrative examples of correct and incorrect output. The prediction errors are **red/bold**.

best model configurations found in Table 3 (layers number = 1, layer dimension = 512).

The first two rows of Table 4 are illustrative examples of categories of intent – snippet pairs that the model can successfully translate. The first row demonstrates the ability of the model to generate multi-line snippets from a relatively abstract intent. The example in the second row shows the model's ability to properly use the instruction `lea` with the correct addressing mode (specified by the bracket [] in NASM syntax) to translate the intent. We note here that although the output would be considered incorrect based on automated metrics (e.g. BLEU-4), it is considered correct using manual inspection.

We also highlight problems with the models through illustrative examples of failure outputs (Rows 3 and 4, Table 4). In the third row of the table, the model generates the wrong instruction due to the model's failure in using implicit knowledge (i.e. the bit-wise inversion to negate the contents of the register) because it was not explicitly mentioned in the intent. Row 4 illustrates the model's failure in predicting the right command among fifteen different conditional jumps in the dataset (`jle` instead of `jge`) in an if-then statement. To summarize, the failures we observed are caused either by a lack of implicit intent knowledge, the model generating incorrect instruction/identifiers (i.e., register names, labels, etc), or even both.

5 Ethical Considerations

Recognizing that attackers use exploit code as a weapon, it is important to specify that the goal of the *proof-of-concept* (POC) exploits is not to cause harm but to surface security weaknesses within the software. Identifying such security issues allows companies to patch vulnerabilities and protect themselves against attacks.

Offensive security is a sub-field of security research that employs ethical hackers to probe a system for vulnerabilities or can be a technique used to disrupt an attacker. *Automatic exploit generation* (AEG), an offensive security technique, is a developing area of research that aims to automate the exploit generation process and to explore and test critical vulnerabilities before they are discovered by attackers (Avgerinos et al., 2014). Indeed, studying exploits on compromised systems can provide valuable information about the technical skills, degree of experience, and intent of the attackers who developed or used them. Using this information, it is possible to implement measures to detect and prevent attacks (Arce, 2004).

6 Conclusion

We address the problem of automated exploit generation through NLP. We use Neural Machine Translation to translate the natural language intents into assembly code. The contribution in this work is a new dataset, *Shellcode_IA32*, containing 3,200 pairs of instructions in assembly language code snippets and their corresponding intents in English. These assembly language snippets can be combined together to generate attacks or exploits on Linux OS running on Intel Architecture 32-bit machines.

Shellcode_IA32 represents a first step towards the ambitious goal of automatically generating shellcodes from natural language. Our experimental evaluation has shown promising early results, demonstrating the feasibility of generating assembly code instructions with high accuracy.

Acknowledgements

This work has been partially supported by the University of Naples Federico II in the frame of the Programme F.R.A., project id OSTAGE.

References

Iván Arce. 2004. The shellcode generation. *IEEE security & privacy*, 2(5):72–76.

Thanassis Avgerinos, Sang Kil Cha, Alexandre Rebert, Edward J. Schwartz, Maverick Woo, and David Brumley. 2014. Automatic exploit generation. *Commun. ACM*, 57(2):74–84.

Dzmitry Bahdanau, Kyunghyun Cho, and Yoshua Bengio. 2015. Neural machine translation by jointly learning to align and translate. *CoRR*, abs/1409.0473.

Tiffany Bao, Ruoyu Wang, Yan Shoshitaishvili, and David Brumley. 2017. Your exploit is mine: Automatic shellcode transplant for remote exploits. In *2017 IEEE Symposium on Security and Privacy (SP)*, pages 824–839. IEEE.

Ondřej Bojar, Rajen Chatterjee, Christian Federmann, Yvette Graham, Barry Haddow, Matthias Huck, Antonio Jimeno Yepes, Philipp Koehn, Varvara Logacheva, Christof Monz, et al. 2016. Findings of the 2016 conference on machine translation. In *Proceedings of the First Conference on Machine Translation: Volume 2, Shared Task Papers*, pages 131–198.

Jeff Duntemann. 2000. *Assembly language step-by-step: programming with DOS and Linux*. John Wiley & Sons.

Jeff Duntemann. 2011. *Assembly language step-by-step: Programming with Linux*. John Wiley & Sons.

Exploit Database Shellcodes . Accessed: 2021-04-22. exploit-db.

Ian Goodfellow, Yoshua Bengio, and Aaron Courville. 2016. *Deep learning*. MIT press.

Kelvin Guu, Panupong Pasupat, Evan Liu, and Percy Liang. 2017. From language to programs: Bridging reinforcement learning and maximum marginal likelihood. In *Proceedings of the 55th Annual Meeting of the Association for Computational Linguistics (Volume 1: Long Papers)*, pages 1051–1062.

Lifeng Han. 2016. Machine translation evaluation resources and methods: A survey. *arXiv preprint arXiv:1605.04515*.

Diederik P. Kingma and Jimmy Ba. 2015. Adam: A method for stochastic optimization. In *3rd International Conference on Learning Representations, ICLR 2015, San Diego, CA, USA, May 7-9, 2015, Conference Track Proceedings*.

Daniel Kusswurm. 2014. *Modern X86 Assembly Language Programming*. Springer.

Xi Victoria Lin, Chenglong Wang, Deric Pang, Kevin Vu, and Michael D Ernst. 2017. Program synthesis from natural language using recurrent neural networks. *University of Washington Department of Computer Science and Engineering, Seattle, WA, USA, Tech. Rep. UW-CSE-17-03-01*.

Xi Victoria Lin, Chenglong Wang, Luke Zettlemoyer, and Michael D. Ernst. 2018. NL2Bash: A corpus and semantic parser for natural language interface to the linux operating system. In *Proceedings of the Eleventh International Conference on Language Resources and Evaluation (LREC 2018)*, Miyazaki, Japan. European Language Resources Association (ELRA).

Wang Ling, Edward Grefenstette, Karl Moritz Hermann, Tomás Kociský, Andrew W. Senior, Fumin Wang, and Phil Blunsom. 2016. Latent predictor networks for code generation. *CoRR*, abs/1603.06744.

Zhongxin Liu, Xin Xia, Ahmed E Hassan, David Lo, Zhenchang Xing, and Xinyu Wang. 2018. Neural-machine-translation-based commit message generation: how far are we? In *Proceedings of the 33rd ACM/IEEE International Conference on Automated Software Engineering*, pages 373–384.

Reginald Long, Panupong Pasupat, and Percy Liang. 2016. Simpler context-dependent logical forms via model projections. In *Proceedings of the 54th Annual Meeting of the Association for Computational Linguistics (Volume 1: Long Papers)*, pages 1456–1465.

Joshua Mason, Sam Small, Fabian Monrose, and Greg MacManus. 2009. English shellcode. In *Proceedings of the 16th ACM conference on Computer and communications security*, pages 524–533.

Dasa Munkova, Petr Hajek, Michal Munk, and Jan Skalka. 2020. Evaluation of machine translation quality through the metrics of error rate and accuracy. *Procedia Computer Science*, 171:1327–1336.

Graham Neubig, Matthias Sperber, Xinyi Wang, Matthieu Felix, Austin Matthews, Sarguna Padmanabhan, Ye Qi, Devendra Sachan, Philip Arthur, Pierre Godard, John Hewitt, Rachid Riad, and Liming Wang. 2018. XNMT: The eXtensible neural machine translation toolkit. In *Proceedings of the 13th Conference of the Association for Machine Translation in the Americas (Volume 1: Research Track)*, pages 185–192, Boston, MA. Association for Machine Translation in the Americas.

Yusuke Oda, Hiroyuki Fudaba, Graham Neubig, Hideaki Hata, Sakriani Sakti, Tomoki Toda, and Satoshi Nakamura. 2015. Learning to generate pseudo-code from source code using statistical machine translation (t). In *2015 30th IEEE/ACM International Conference on Automated Software Engineering (ASE)*, pages 574–584. IEEE.

Kishore Papineni, Salim Roukos, Todd Ward, and Wei-Jing Zhu. 2002. Bleu: a method for automatic evaluation of machine translation. In *Proceedings of the 40th annual meeting on association for computational linguistics*, pages 311–318. Association for Computational Linguistics.

pwntools. Accessed: 2021-05-29. *pwntools*.

Shellcodes database for study cases. Accessed: 2021-04-22. shell-storm.

Tutorialspoint. Accessed: 2021-04-22. Assembly Programming Tutorial.

Yonghui Wu, Mike Schuster, Zhifeng Chen, Quoc V. Le, Mohammad Norouzi, Wolfgang Macherey, Maxim Krikun, Yuan Cao, Qin Gao, Klaus Macherey, Jeff Klingner, Apurva Shah, Melvin Johnson, Xiaobing Liu, Lukasz Kaiser, Stephan Gouws, Yoshikiyo Kato, Taku Kudo, Hideto Kazawa, Keith Stevens, George Kurian, Nishant Patil, Wei Wang, Cliff Young, Jason Smith, Jason Riesa, Alex Rudnick, Oriol Vinyals, Greg Corrado, Macduff Hughes, and Jeffrey Dean. 2016. Google's neural machine translation system: Bridging the gap between human and machine translation. *CoRR*, abs/1609.08144.

Frank F. Xu, Zhengbao Jiang, Pengcheng Yin, Bogdan Vasilescu, and Graham Neubig. 2020. Incorporating external knowledge through pre-training for natural language to code generation. In *Proceedings of the 58th Annual Meeting of the Association for Computational Linguistics*, pages 6045–6052, Online. Association for Computational Linguistics.

Pengcheng Yin, Bowen Deng, Edgar Chen, Bogdan Vasilescu, and Graham Neubig. 2018. Learning to mine aligned code and natural language pairs from stack overflow. In *International Conference on Mining Software Repositories*, MSR, pages 476–486. ACM.

Pengcheng Yin and Graham Neubig. 2017. A syntactic neural model for general-purpose code generation. *CoRR*, abs/1704.01696.

Pengcheng Yin and Graham Neubig. 2019. Reranking for neural semantic parsing. In *Proceedings of the 57th Annual Meeting of the Association for Computational Linguistics*, pages 4553–4559.

Reading StackOverflow Encourages Cheating: Adding Question Text Improves Extractive Code Generation

Gabriel Orlanski
Rensselaer Polytechnic Institute
orlang2@rpi.edu

Alex Gittens
Rensselaer Polytechnic Institute
gittea@rpi.edu

Abstract

Answering a programming question using only its title is difficult as salient contextual information is omitted. Based on this observation, we present a corpus of over 40,000 StackOverflow question texts to be used in conjunction with their corresponding intents from the CoNaLa dataset (Yin et al., 2018). Using both the intent and question body, we use BART to establish a baseline BLEU score of 34.35 for this new task. We find further improvements of 2.8% by combining the mined CoNaLa data with the labeled data to achieve a 35.32 BLEU score. We evaluate prior state-of-the-art CoNaLa models with this additional data and find that our proposed method of using the body and mined data beats the BLEU score of the prior state-of-the-art by 71.96%. Finally, we perform ablations to demonstrate that BART is an unsupervised multimodal learner and examine its extractive behavior.[1]

1 Introduction

The goal of semantic parsing is to translate a Natural Language(NL) utterance to its logical components. There is a large body of research on applying semantic parsing for source code generation in a multitude of domain specific languages such as lambda calculus and SQL (Dahl et al., 1994; Zelle and Mooney, 1996; Zettlemoyer and Collins, 2005; Ling et al., 2016; Xiao et al., 2016; Rabinovich et al., 2017; Dong and Lapata, 2018; Guo et al., 2019; Hwang et al., 2019; Tabassum et al., 2020). However, the task of translating an NL utterance to a general-purpose programming language has proven to be more challenging. A significant issue contributing to this is the difficulty in acquiring quality data due to the necessary domain knowledge needed in the annotation process.

Despite this, the past few years have seen a large number of datasets released for different text-to-

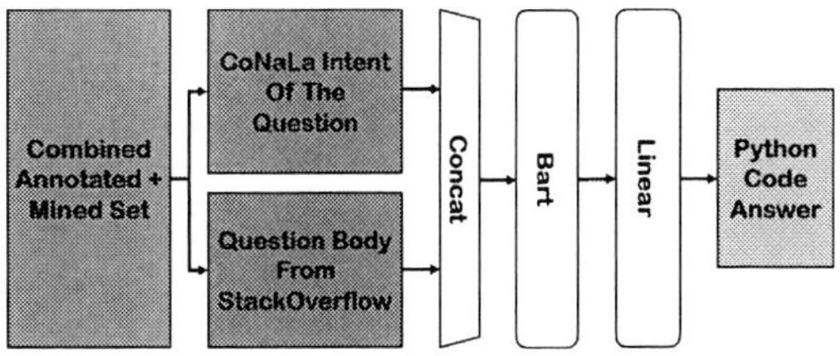

Figure 1: Overview of our approach. From the combined annotated + mined set, we concatenate the intent and question body for inputs to BART(Lewis et al., 2020) and use beam search for generation.

code related tasks (Ling et al., 2016; Iyer et al., 2018; Yao et al., 2018; Yu et al., 2018; Lu et al., 2021). Some datasets such as CodeSearchNet (Husain et al., 2019) contain snippets from a multitude of different languages. Others focus on distinct tasks within a specific language, such as JuICe (Agashe et al., 2019), which contains executable Python programming assignments. Utilizing these corpora, prior works (Suhr et al., 2018; Yin and Neubig, 2017, 2018; Sun et al., 2019; Hayati et al., 2018; Yin and Neubig, 2019; Xu et al., 2020; Drain et al., 2021) have found success with a large variety of model architectures. These methods, however, struggle with domain agnostic open-ended code generation in general-purpose languages. One idea to combat this is to utilize large pretrained language models.

Transformers (Vaswani et al., 2017) have demonstrated that they can both be few-shot (Brown et al., 2020) and unsupervised multitask (Radford et al., 2019) learners. They have been successfully applied to programming language tasks. CodeBERT achieved strong performance on the CodeSearchNet task through pretraining on bimodal NL comment and code pairs(Feng et al., 2020), while Sun et al. (2019) used abstract syntax trees(AST) and transformers to achieve state of the art performance on the HearthStone benchmark(Ling et al., 2016). Roziere et al. (2021) proposed the deobfuscation

[1] https://github.com/gabeorlanski/stackoverflow-encourages-cheating

Proceedings of the 1st Workshop on Natural Language Processing for Programming (NLP4Prog 2021), pages 65–76
August 1–6, 2021.

pretraining task to incorporate structural features of code into transformer models without the use of ASTs. More recently, Shin et al. (2021) explored the capabilities of large pretrained language models to be few-shot semantic parsers.

Yet open-domain programming question answering on sites such as StackOverflow(SO)[2] has remained an elusive goal. Yin et al. (2018) created an annotated dataset with the site in which the intent and answer snippet pairs were automatically mined from the question. They then had crowd workers rewrite the intents to reflect the corresponding code better. Currently, state-of-the-art was achieved by pretraining an LSTM model on resampled API and mined data (Xu et al., 2020). Subsequent work conducted an empirical study on the effectiveness of using a code generation model in an IDE plugin and find that developers largely had favorable opinions of their experience(Xu et al., 2021). An inherent issue with the approach of Xu et al. (2020), more fundamentally the dataset and parameters of the task, is that the intent can only contain a limited amount of information.

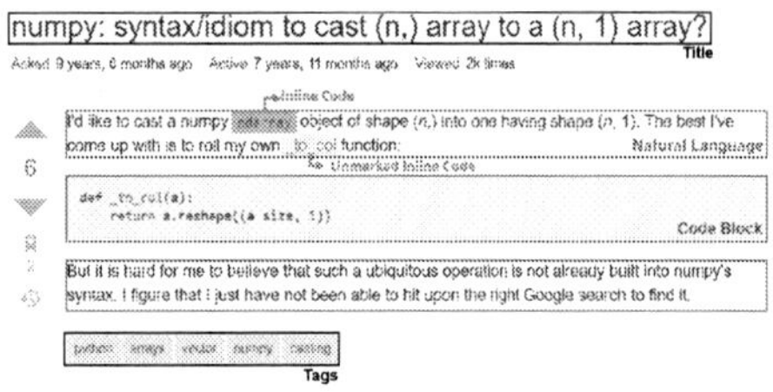

Figure 2: Example StackOverflow question with labeled elements. The corresponding rewritten intent for this question is "add a new axis to array `a`."

Consider the question from Figure 2 in which a valid python snippet could be `a[:, (np.newaxis)]`. Arriving at this answer from the intent "add a new axis to array `a`" requires not only the disambiguation of data types for variable `a`, but also the use of multiple distinct library-specific concepts. Further, this must be accomplished while maintaining syntactically correct code and proper order of arguments. However, neither the original title nor the rewritten intent contains the necessary information to accomplish this task. Although the previous state-of-the-art-model by Xu et al. (2020) uses abstract syntax trees (AST) to guarantee syntactically valid python code, it incorrectly generates `a[(-1),:]=a`. One potential remedy would be to increase the amount of training data, but as discussed previously, getting high-quality annotated code generation data is especially difficult.

Motivated by the limitations to the amount of information a given intent can contain and the substantial difficulty involved with gathering more labeled data, we utilize the multimodal text from the question bodies provided by the StackExchange API[3]. We take advantage of the strong performances of transformer models to beat the previous state-of-the-art by 3.06 BLEU. We ensure a fair comparison by training the models from prior works with the extra data to adequately evaluate our proposed method. When all models are trained with the extra data, using BART beats the previous state of the art by 15.12 BLEU.

Our main contributions are the following:

- Expanding upon the original CoNaLa dataset (Yin et al., 2018) to include the multimodal textual question bodies and thus the pertinent contextual information they contain such as inputs, outputs, and required libraries.
- Demonstrating that BART does not rely on a single modality, but rather achieves its best performance on our dataset when all modalities are included. This indicates at least a shallow understanding of both natural and programming language as well as how they are related in the context of SO questions.
- Conducting experiments revealing that BART's struggle to generate syntacically correct code is likely a result of its tendency to be extractive rather than generative in the task of text-to-code generation.

2 Methodology

As detailed in Figure 1, our overarching approach is to: *(1)* gather textual bodies from SO for both the annotated and mined examples in the CoNaLa corpus, *(2)* use the concatenated intents and question bodies as inputs for a large pretrained language model, and *(3)* use beam search to generate the answer code snippet.

2.1 StackOverflow Data

Every example $e_i \in E$ from the CoNaLa dataset (Yin et al., 2018) is comprised of an intent $x_i \in X$ that concisely summarizes what the poster wants

[2]https://stackoverflow.com/

[3]https://api.stackexchange.com/

and a snippet of Python code $y_i \in Y$ that represents an implementation of x_i. Crowd sourcing was used to rewrite a selection of the mined intents to reflect the snippet better and to ensure that the snippet was indeed a correct answer. As discussed, these intents are limited in the amount of information they can contain. The intent "add a new axis to array `a`" from Figure 2 could refer to a wide variety of different Python objects. It could range from the default `list` to the `Tensor` object from PyTorch[4]. The full question, or either its tags or title, is typically enough for a human to disambiguate the correct library to use. But the annotated intent lacks this crucial information as it is rather difficult to design an annotation task for SO data.[5]

We address this problem directly by using the additional data found in the SO question. In Figure 2 there are four direct mentions of the NumPy library: two in the question body and one each in both the tags and the title. Further, there is a direct mention of the `ndarray` data type from NumPy. It is, therefore, rather intuitive to include this additional data as input with the hope that it improves the answer generation performance. Although we did mention that both the tags and title provide salient information, the focus of this paper is only on using the noisy textual question bodies. Therefore, for every example e_i the inputs now become the concatenation of x_i and the body $q_{x_i} \in Q$ from the original SO question. It is important to note that $|Q| \neq |E|$ as a single question can have many examples while every question is, by definition, unique.

2.2 Unsupervised Modality Learning

Multiple modalities are present in the textual body of a given question. These can range from embedded images to messages from administrators (or upset users) stating that the question is a duplicate of some tangentially related post that does not have an answer. While these are useful to readers, we limit our focus to three modalities: code blocks, inline code, and NL. These modalities are marked in Figure 2 with blue, green, and red, respectively. Ideally, we would prefer to leave in the HTML tags to serve as sentinel tokens, but, looking at Figure 2, one immediately finds that the poster forgot to mark `_to_col` as inline code. Therefore, we remove all HTML tags from the inputs, creating an unsupervised learning environment. Therefore, we propose that a transformer model will learn each of the three modalities and learn to use the relationships between each. We use BART(Lewis et al., 2020) because its pretraining focuses on denoising textual data and, to the best of our knowledge, has minimal exposure to code examples. We used HuggingFace's (Wolf et al., 2020) `BartForConditionalGeneration` model which has a default BART encoder-decoder model with a linear layer and bias for outputs.

2.3 Unlabeled Data

We followed Xu et al. (2020) by using large amounts of the mined but not annotated data. Unlike Xu et al. (2020), however, we do not use this data for pretraining. Instead, we combine this data with the annotated data in our main training and validation sets. By adding more questions to the training set, we directly increase the probability that the model encounters a larger and more representative distribution of libraries. Intuitively, this will reduce the variances between experiments as we have reduced the dependency on the specific examples used in the training and validation sets. This variance reduction is especially useful when working with a small dataset such as CoNaLa.

3 Experiments

3.1 Datasets

CoNaLa (Yin et al., 2018)[6] is an open domain text to code generation task constructed from SO questions. It has 2,879[7] annotated NL-code pairs with more than 590K mined pairs from over 40,000 unique SO questions in the dataset.

StackOverflow Data For every unique question in both the annotated and mined sets, we gather additional data from the StackExchange API. As discussed in subsection 2.1, we only use the question body as input. Therefore the task is to generate a valid answer snippet from both the intent and the textual body. Detailed statistics for this dataset are given in Table 1 and Table 2.

3.2 Methods

We removed 238 (10%) examples from the training set to form the validation set. We then followed Xu et al. (2020) in taking the top mined samples based on their given probability that the NL-Code pair

[4]https://pytorch.org/

[5]We direct readers to Yin et al. (2018) for a full discussion of these challenges.

[6]https://conala-corpus.github.io/

[7]Actual Number is lower due to errors in the dataset preventing the usage of some examples.

Split	$\|E\|^*$	$\|Q\|^*$	$\|E\|/\|Q\|$ ①	Intent Tokens ②	Snippet Tokens ②	Body Tokens ③
Train	2376	1708	1.39±1.02	16.45±7.51	17.23±8.58	221.90±202.65
Test	498	364	1.37±0.88	15.98±6.62	18.47±12.90	208.04±164.74
Mined-10K	9988†	7181	1.39±0.80	11.29±3.94	16.58±9.27	297.53±367.09
Mined	593837	40522	14.65±7.01	11.41±4.22	28.70±42.81	371.24±483.67

Table 1: Statistics for the CoNaLa dataset with data from the StackOverflow API. $|E|$ is # of examples. $|Q|$ number of questions. Values are reported as $\mu \pm \sigma$ unless the column header has *. ①Mean # of examples for a Question. ②Per example. ③ Number of tokens in the body regardless of modalitiy. †12 of the 10K questions were removed because there was an issue with them.

Split	Have Answer*	Has Code	Inline ①	Blocks ①	Code Tokens ①	NL Tokens ①
Train	87.88%	85.95%	1.21±2.09	1.42±1.26	95.54±157.52	124.60±92.02
Test	87.09%	87.91%	1.08±1.87	1.50±1.26	88.21±116.01	118.52±79.51
Mined-10K	86.16%	84.00%	1.30±2.36	1.46±1.34	133.20±278.20	164.54±207.08
Mined	81.92%	81.83%	1.50±2.86	1.47±1.44	172.57±372.32	197.98±257.71

Table 2: Detailed statistics for the StackOverflow questions. Mined-10K represents the top 10,000 samples selected from the Mined data based on their probability that they are a valid NL-Code pair. *Percent of questions that have an accepted answer. ①Per question body.

is valid. However, we only used 10,000 samples rather than the 100,000 Xu et al. (2020) used. From this, we remove 1000 for validation.[8] For all tests of our model with the mined data, we combine the two training and validation sets into one.

Every experiment and test conducted in this work was conducting using Google's Colab Pro service. It afforded us the ability to use 512 input tokens with a batch size of 16. More importantly, we were able to use P100 and V100 graphics cards. Following that, we perform an ablation study using BART and the different components of our approach. Every ablation is run five separate times with different seeds and validation splits. For each test, the model with the lowest validation loss is used in the evaluation. Each test is run for ten epochs as we consistently observed overfitting after five to eight epochs.

Because we introduce new data at inference, we needed to ensure we fairly compare our methods with previous work. To this end, we run the prior works with the question bodies as inputs. However, for testing Xu et al. (2020) with the question bodies, we limited the amount of mined data in pretraining to 10,000 instead of 100,000. This was done due to Google Colab's execution time limits, as it took upwards of four hours for each run of Xu et al. (2020) with only 10,000 samples.

[8]Some questions were deleted from StackOverflow in both the annotated and mined sets, so we could not use those.

3.3 Metrics

We measure the corpus level BLEU score of the generated code snippets with the same postprocessing methods and smoothing as Xu et al. (2020). We evaluate our ablations by comparing the corpus BLEU score and unigram, bigram, and trigram precision. Finally, we calculate the percentage of test examples for which our model generated a syntactically valid Python snippet.

For the previous state-of-the-art, we also report the Oracle BLEU proposed by Yin and Neubig (2019). This is calculated by choosing the candidate snippet s_i with the highest sentence level BLEU score out of n generated snippets. Formally, given the candidate list $C = [c_1, \ldots, c_n]$ and ground truth y_i,

$$z = \underset{c_j \in C}{\text{argmax}}\ \text{BLEU}(c_j, y_i) \tag{1}$$

Furthermore, we want to quantify how much our model relies on the body of the question or "cheats." To do this, we calculate the cheating for the generated snippet $s_i \in [s_1, \ldots, s_N] = S$ and ground truth $y_i \in [y_1, \ldots, y_N] = Y$ with respect to the input text $b_i \in [b_1, \ldots, b_N] = B$. Given the function $m(a, b)$ that calculates a textual similarity metric m, we define the cheating w.r.t. m as

$$C_m(S) = \frac{\sum_{i \in [1;N]} (m(s_i, b_i) - m(y_i, b_i))}{N} \tag{2}$$

If the model is heavily "cheating" from the input, then $m(s_i, b_i) \gg m(y_i, b_i)$, which leads to a large

C_m. The quantity C_m is, by design, similar to a standard mean squared error. The largest difference is that the difference is not squared, to facilitate distinguishing between less and more similar.

For the metric function m, we use BLEU and ROUGE (Lin, 2004). For the former, we take the bigram (C_{BB}) and trigram (C_{BT}) precision from BLEU. For ROUGE, we use bigram ROUGE (ROUGE-2/C_{R2}) and the longest common subsequence (ROUGE-L/C_{RL}). The intuition behind using these metrics is that there is a high probability that unigram precision is large. The answers to a question must address the contents of the said question, leading to shared tokens between inputs and outputs. However, the probability should massively drop when considering multiple grams. Therefore, the similarity between n-grams when $n > 1$ should indicate the reliance on the inputs.

3.4 Implementation

We implemented our model with Python and HuggingFace's transformer library (Wolf et al., 2020)[9]. We used a BART model with a linear layer and a separate bias for text generation. We utilized the smallest available BART model from FAIR, which was the Facebook/BART-base[10]. For training, we again rely on HuggingFace's trainer and their implementation of the learning rate scheduler. We used Adam (Loshchilov and Hutter, 2017) as our optimizer with a learning rate of 5e−5 and a linear learning rate scheduler. We also used a warmup ratio of 0.05. Finally, for generation, we used beam search with four beams, early stopping, and a length penalty of 0.9.

4 Results

We list the previous state-of-the-art BLEU scores for the CoNaLa dataset as well as the performance of our models in Table 3. Using the intent and question bodies achieved a BLEU score of 34.35±1.01. This was further increased to 35.32±0.42 by including the mined data in the training and validation set. To better understand our model, we perform ablation tests and report their results in Table 4. When comparing our top performance with the previous top performance, regardless of the data used, our model beats the previous state of the art by 3.40 BLEU, a 10.54% increase. Notably, our model outperforms the previous SoTA by 14.78 BLEU, a 71.96% increase when only comparing the experiments with the question body. Furthermore, BART with the mined data and question bodies beats their Oracle BLEU by 1.61 BLEU, translating to a 4.78% increase. However, it is important to note that Xu et al. (2020) outperforms our model by 1.71(5.30%) when we do not use the textual body. But they still both beat the baseline TranX by 25.72% and 7.98%, respectively. The use of the mined data further beat the reranker by 1.46%.

The 71.96% increase is likely because TranX models were never intended to perform well with very noisy data, as evidenced by the 36% dropoff in corpus BLEU when adding the body to Xu et al. (2020). In choosing BART, we intentionally picked a transformer model designed for denoising (Lewis et al., 2020). Further testing is likely needed to determine if our approach is heavily dependent on the underlying transformer, but that is beyond the scope of this paper.

4.1 Impact of adding the Question Body

Adding the body of the question objectively improved the performance of the model. The BLEU score increased 30.92% to 34.35 and, per Table 4, there was an increase across unigram, bigram, and trigram precision. While they all do increase, the amount is far from constant. The unigram precision only saw a 3.61% increase, whereas bigram and trigram precision increased by 12.77% and 22.90%, respectively. This indicates that while the model selected slightly more correct tokens, it greatly improved its ordering of said tokens.

Similar improvements, albeit smaller in value, also occurred when including the mined data without the question bodies. However, there was a sharp drop in the standard deviations for the three precision metrics. In contrast, adding the question body resulted in a steep increase in variance. This is most probably a result of the "shrinking" of the dataset that occurred when we added the bodies. In Table 1 we report that *every* split of the dataset has fewer unique questions than it does examples. Also reported is that the number of tokens in the body is, on average, significantly greater than that of the intents. The effective dataset size is now much smaller, while the number of unique answer snippets stayed the same. The result is that the model now performs better on the difficult test set, at the cost of being more reliant on the training and validation split. Using both the bodies and mined

[9] https://github.com/huggingface/transformers

[10] https://huggingface.co/facebook/bart-base

Model	No Body Corpus BLEU	With Body Corpus BLEU	 Oracle BLEU
TranX (Yin and Neubig, 2018)	24.30	18.85±1.26	31.21±0.30
RR (Yin and Neubig, 2019)	30.11	19.85±1.21	31.21±0.30
EK (Xu et al., 2020)	30.69	20.37±1.44	33.71±0.83
EK+RR(Xu et al., 2020)	**32.26**	20.54±0.85	33.71±0.83
BART	26.24±0.31①	34.35±1.01	≥ 34.35
BART W/ Mined	30.55±0.38①	**35.32**±0.42	≥ 35.32

Table 3: Results compared to previous papers both with and without the use of the question body at inference. We do not calculate the Oracle BLEU for either of our models as our corpus BLEU already surpasses their Oracle BLEU. EK=Using External Knowledge. RR=Using Reranking. ①Using only the rewritten intent, if available else normal intent, as input.

data does mitigate this "shrinking" effect, as shown by the lower standard deviations than those when only using the body.

4.2 Is BART Reliant on a Single Modality

As discussed in subsection 2.2, we focus on three modalities in the textual bodies: code blocks, inline code, and natural language. We put forth the idea that a large pretrained language model such as BART learns each modality in an unsupervised manner. We designed four distinct ablations to test if this was the case. Each was run both with and without the mined data totaling eight ablations. We report the full BLEU scores from these in Table 4. Further, we calculate the performance with respect to baselines in Table 5. Notably, there was no modality whose removal resulted in a BLEU score worse than when the question body was not used in the input. There was also not a modality whose removal improved performance. From our ablations, it is clear that the most important modality in the question bodies is the code regardless of if it is inline or in a block. But, using only code is still 2.25% worse than when all three modalities are included with mined. This indicates that the NL surrounding acts not only as additional context, but likely further both direct and indirect indicators of salient code for the model.

4.3 Removing Code Improves Syntax

In Table 4 we report the percent of generated snippets that are syntactically valid—adding only the mined data results in a 9% increase. When using the question bodies, the addition of the mined data also increases the percent of valid snippets generated by 7.88%. While it is an improvement, it is still a 3.76% drop from when the body was excluded. Further, removing the code from the bodies resulted in the highest percentages of 92.00% and 84.92% with and without the mined data. We then performed a finer analysis using a single seed and the same training and validation data across all ablations and reported the results in Appendix A. Across all ablations, the majority of errors are caused by mismatches of parentheses. In reality, a large percentage of general syntax errors are likely caused by this. However, syntax errors prevent the extraction of the AST for further investigation of these errors.

We also report in Table 9 the percentage of valid snippets generated when the `print` function is present. One of the more commonly occurring incompatibilities between Python 2 and 3 is that `print` now requires parentheses. Considering that the questions in the CoNaLa dataset are from March 2017 or earlier (Yin et al., 2018) and that support for Python 2.x only ended in January 2020[11], we hypothesize that these deprecated calls are a large cause of the errors. When both the body and snippet have `print`, the inclusion of the question body led to the percent of valid snippets dropping by 21.06 with and 21.05 without the mined data with respect to their baselines. While there are only 19 such questions in the test set, this is a significant drop. The likely cause is that the autoregressive decoder of BART struggles to remember to close the parentheses when wrapping the snippet with a `print` statement. One solution would be to run the `2to3`[12] translator on all of the code. However, the possibilities for code blocks to contain code and other modalities such as error messages and console executions present significant hurdles

[11]https://www.python.org/doc/sunset-python-2/
[12]https://docs.python.org/3/library/2to3.html

Input	BLEU	Unigram*	Bigram*	Trigram*	Valid①
Baseline	26.24±0.31	67.53±0.46	44.10±0.60	29.80±0.69	84.08±1.27
+Mined	30.55±0.38	67.81±0.23	45.55±0.27	31.69±0.37	**93.08**±1.28
Body	34.35±1.01	69.97±0.89	**49.74**±0.99	**36.62**±0.97	81.44±2.25
-NL	34.06±0.48	68.29±0.48	47.91±0.45	35.33±0.40	81.92±0.75
-Code	27.67±0.40	68.29±0.53	44.93±0.57	30.12±0.69	84.92±1.00
-Blocks	29.53±0.47	68.14±0.26	45.69±0.10	31.36±0.15	80.84±1.37
-Inline	33.57±0.94	**70.50**±0.27	49.56±0.40	36.54±0.46	82.16±1.53
Body+Mined	**35.32**±0.42	67.62±0.76	47.69±0.82	35.00±0.87	89.32±1.49
-NL	34.53±0.88	66.24±0.90	46.11±1.15	33.54±1.02	90.08±0.48
-Code	31.39±0.75	67.00±0.75	45.65±0.97	31.60±0.88	92.00±1.31
-Blocks	32.14±0.14	66.96±1.03	45.32±0.97	31.49±0.74	89.24±1.30
-Inline	35.06±0.49	67.04±1.54	46.99±1.29	34.31±1.04	89.20±0.42

Table 4: Ablation Experiments all with BART ran on 5 different random initializations. All tests have rewritten intent as input in addition to the input described in the **Input** column. The **bolded ablation** indicates our best performance while red text represents the worst performance. *Precisions. ①Percent of generated snippets that are valid python.

	Body	Body+Mined
-NL	-0.29	-0.80
-Code	-6.68	-3.93
-Blocks	-4.83	-3.18
-Inline	-0.79	-0.26

Table 5: Change in BLEU score for each ablation versus their respective baseline.

as `2to3` does not support these. Therefore we leave that to future work.

4.4 Cheating

In subsection 3.3 we define the "cheating" equation to measure if the generated snippet is more similar to the question body than the ground truth is. The ideal model would maximize the BLEU score while minimizing the $|C_m|$. We run multiple ablations on a single seed and calculate the "cheating" as defined by Equation 2 and present these results in Table 6.

Suffice to say that *serious* violations of academic integrity have occurred. As expected, the baseline is less similar to the question bodies than the ground truth is. When the body was used as input, C_{BT} increased by 20.28 points, while C_{RL} rose by 3.16 points, representing a 293.49% and 159.60% increase over their respective baselines. Including the mined data resulted in increases of 18.59 (308.13%) and 0.77(265.52%) when compared to using only the intents. Both indicate that the model's generated output has significantly more shared multigram subsequences with the question body than the ground truth does. In the ablations where code was removed from the body, C_{BT} increased by only 0.98 and 1.86 with and without the mined data. This represents a percent of increase of only 16.25% and 26.92% over their respective baselines. However, in the case where all NL was removed, C_{BT} increased by 17.35(287.73%) and 19.18(277.57%) points with respect to their baselines. The fact that these increases are lower than that when all modalities are included provides further evidence that BART is an unsupervised mul-

	C_{BB}	C_{BT}	C_{R2}	C_{RL}
Baseline	-6.82	-6.91	-1.62	-1.98
+Mined	-6.03	-6.03	-1.41	-0.29
Body	11.65	13.37	1.75	1.18
-Code	-4.18	-5.05	-1.06	-1.40
-NL	10.55	12.27	1.24	0.47
-Blocks	-3.32	-3.48	-0.89	-1.09
-Inline	9.19	10.39	0.90	0.44
Body+Mined	10.19	12.55	1.39	0.48
-Code	-4.37	-5.05	-1.08	-1.47
-NL	9.40	11.32	1.19	0.17
-Blocks	-3.48	-4.16	-0.84	-1.19
-Inline	7.93	9.73	1.11	0.25

Table 6: Cheating Measurements calculated by Equation 2 using a single run but same seed and environment. C_{BB} and C_{BT} are the cheating w.r.t. BLEU Bigram and Trigram Precision. C_{R2} and C_{RL} are the cheating w.r.t. ROUGE-2 and ROUGE-L.

timodal learner and understands the relationships between each modality. The NL likely provides both explicit and implicit hints about the importance of certain code spans.

4.5 Examples

Intent: multiply a matrix 'p' with a 3d tensor 't' in scipy
✓ `scipy.tensordot(P, T, axes=[1, 1]).swapaxes(0, 1)`
① `np.einsum('...j,...j->...', P, T)`
② `np.einsum('ij->ij->ik->j->ik', p)`
① `P.dot(T).transpose(1, 0, 2)`
Intent: concatenate items of list 'l' with a space ' '
✓ `print(' '.join(map(str, l)))`
① `list(map(tuple, []))`
② `[item for item in L if '' in item]`
③ `print(' '.join(str(x) for x in L))`
Intent: concatenate elements of list 'b' by a colon ":"
✓ `""":""".join(str(x) for x in b)`
① `[' '.join(x) for x in b]`
② `b = [int(i) for i in b]`
③ `print(':'.join(map(str, b)))`

Table 7: Example intents and generated snippets. Screenshots of the questions are located in Appendix B and each intent links to the question. Red text indicates that it is incorrect while blue text marks correct tokens in the wrong place. ✓ground truth. ①EK+RR no body (Xu et al., 2020). ②Mined. ③Body+Mined.

We select three examples that demonstrate the benefits of our approach while also highlighting the issues in both the use of the question body and SO corpora in general and report them in Table 7. In the first example, we can see that both ① and ② have learned how to use einsums, but neither is correct. ③ in this case produces an answer that returns the correct value. It is highly probable that BART understood from the poster's explicit mention that `P.dot(T).transpose(1, 0, 2)` gives the desired result and thus extracts it. However, this example has two critical issues: the poster's intent is to find a "cleaner" way to multiply a matrix with a tensor, and `scipy.tensordot` is deprecated. The latter is to be expected, considering the answer is from 2010. But it does indicate that a better evaluation based on inputs and outputs is likely needed.

The next two examples are quite similar but are from two separate questions. ① likely mistakes the core intent to be type conversion due to the inclusion of the words "items" and "with." ② also suffers from the inclusion of these tokens but believes the problem involves filtering. In the final example, ① recognizes that it must convert the items in `b` to `str`, but does not return a joined string. ② recognizes that, again, the answer involves type conversion but predicts the incorrect type.

Similar to the first example, ③ produces answers for both the second and third examples that functionally return the correct results. However, running ③'s solution for the third example would result in a syntax error due to the missing "`)`." On further inspection of the question bodies, it becomes apparent that the probable reason why one snippet is syntactically valid while the other is not is the presence of a Python 2 `print`. The model recognizes that a suitable answer can be found in the question but must be converted to python 3. As discussed in subsection 4.3, these print statements are prone to cause syntactical issues.

5 Conclusion

We expand the CoNaLa dataset by adding the textual question bodies from the StackExchange API and achieve state-of-the-art performance with a simple BART model. Further, we demonstrate that, for this task, BART performs best when code blocks, inline code, and NL are all present. We then examine the impact of the question body on syntax errors and BART's cheating through multimodal understanding. Finally, we examine examples that highlight the issues with both StackOverflow data and code evaluation in general. Future work should focus on extracting desired inputs and outputs for a given intent. Further, additional efforts put into creating corpora of executable code are likely to improve not only generation but evaluation. Both will also protect datasets from deprecated functions and abandoned libraries.

References

Rajas Agashe, Srinivasan Iyer, and Luke Zettlemoyer. 2019. JuICe: A large scale distantly supervised dataset for open domain context-based code generation. In *Proceedings of the 2019 Conference on Empirical Methods in Natural Language Processing and the 9th International Joint Conference on Natural Language Processing (EMNLP-IJCNLP)*, pages 5436–5446, Hong Kong, China. Association for Computational Linguistics.

Tom B. Brown, Benjamin Mann, Nick Ryder, Melanie Subbiah, Jared Kaplan, Prafulla Dhariwal, Arvind Neelakantan, Pranav Shyam, Girish Sastry, Amanda

Askell, Sandhini Agarwal, Ariel Herbert-Voss, Gretchen Krueger, Tom Henighan, Rewon Child, Aditya Ramesh, Daniel M. Ziegler, Jeffrey Wu, Clemens Winter, Christopher Hesse, Mark Chen, Eric Sigler, Mateusz Litwin, Scott Gray, Benjamin Chess, Jack Clark, Christopher Berner, Sam McCandlish, Alec Radford, Ilya Sutskever, and Dario Amodei. 2020. Language models are few-shot learners.

Deborah A. Dahl, Madeleine Bates, Michael Brown, William Fisher, Kate Hunicke-Smith, David Pallett, Christine Pao, Alexander Rudnicky, and Elizabeth Shriberg. 1994. Expanding the scope of the ATIS task: The ATIS-3 corpus. In *Human Language Technology: Proceedings of a Workshop held at Plainsboro, New Jersey, March 8-11, 1994.*

Li Dong and Mirella Lapata. 2018. Coarse-to-fine decoding for neural semantic parsing. In *Proceedings of the 56th Annual Meeting of the Association for Computational Linguistics (Volume 1: Long Papers)*, pages 731–742, Melbourne, Australia. Association for Computational Linguistics.

Dawn Drain, Changran Hu, Chen Wu, Mikhail Breslav, and Neel Sundaresan. 2021. Generating code with the help of retrieved template functions and stack overflow answers.

Zhangyin Feng, Daya Guo, Duyu Tang, Nan Duan, Xiaocheng Feng, Ming Gong, Linjun Shou, Bing Qin, Ting Liu, Daxin Jiang, and Ming Zhou. 2020. CodeBERT: A pre-trained model for programming and natural languages. In *Findings of the Association for Computational Linguistics: EMNLP 2020*, pages 1536–1547, Online. Association for Computational Linguistics.

Jiaqi Guo, Zecheng Zhan, Yan Gao, Yan Xiao, Jian-Guang Lou, Ting Liu, and Dongmei Zhang. 2019. Towards complex text-to-SQL in cross-domain database with intermediate representation. In *Proceedings of the 57th Annual Meeting of the Association for Computational Linguistics*, pages 4524–4535, Florence, Italy. Association for Computational Linguistics.

Shirley Anugrah Hayati, Raphael Olivier, Pravalika Avvaru, Pengcheng Yin, Anthony Tomasic, and Graham Neubig. 2018. Retrieval-based neural code generation. In *Proceedings of the 2018 Conference on Empirical Methods in Natural Language Processing*, pages 925–930, Brussels, Belgium. Association for Computational Linguistics.

Hamel Husain, Ho-Hsiang Wu, Tiferet Gazit, Miltiadis Allamanis, and Marc Brockschmidt. 2019. Codesearchnet challenge: Evaluating the state of semantic code search. *arXiv preprint arXiv:1909.09436*.

Wonseok Hwang, Jinyeong Yim, Seunghyun Park, and Minjoon Seo. 2019. A comprehensive exploration on wikisql with table-aware word contextualization.

Srinivasan Iyer, Ioannis Konstas, Alvin Cheung, and Luke Zettlemoyer. 2018. Mapping language to code in programmatic context. In *Proceedings of the 2018 Conference on Empirical Methods in Natural Language Processing*, pages 1643–1652, Brussels, Belgium. Association for Computational Linguistics.

Mike Lewis, Yinhan Liu, Naman Goyal, Marjan Ghazvininejad, Abdelrahman Mohamed, Omer Levy, Veselin Stoyanov, and Luke Zettlemoyer. 2020. BART: Denoising sequence-to-sequence pre-training for natural language generation, translation, and comprehension. In *Proceedings of the 58th Annual Meeting of the Association for Computational Linguistics*, pages 7871–7880, Online. Association for Computational Linguistics.

Chin-Yew Lin. 2004. ROUGE: A package for automatic evaluation of summaries. In *Text Summarization Branches Out*, pages 74–81, Barcelona, Spain. Association for Computational Linguistics.

Wang Ling, Phil Blunsom, Edward Grefenstette, Karl Moritz Hermann, Tomáš Kočiský, Fumin Wang, and Andrew Senior. 2016. Latent predictor networks for code generation. In *Proceedings of the 54th Annual Meeting of the Association for Computational Linguistics (Volume 1: Long Papers)*, pages 599–609, Berlin, Germany. Association for Computational Linguistics.

Ilya Loshchilov and Frank Hutter. 2017. Fixing weight decay regularization in adam. *CoRR*, abs/1711.05101.

Shuai Lu, Daya Guo, Shuo Ren, Junjie Huang, Alexey Svyatkovskiy, Ambrosio Blanco, Colin B. Clement, Dawn Drain, Daxin Jiang, Duyu Tang, Ge Li, Lidong Zhou, Linjun Shou, Long Zhou, Michele Tufano, Ming Gong, Ming Zhou, Nan Duan, Neel Sundaresan, Shao Kun Deng, Shengyu Fu, and Shujie Liu. 2021. Codexglue: A machine learning benchmark dataset for code understanding and generation. *CoRR*, abs/2102.04664.

Maxim Rabinovich, Mitchell Stern, and Dan Klein. 2017. Abstract syntax networks for code generation and semantic parsing. In *Proceedings of the 55th Annual Meeting of the Association for Computational Linguistics (Volume 1: Long Papers)*, pages 1139–1149, Vancouver, Canada. Association for Computational Linguistics.

Alec Radford, Jeffrey Wu, Rewon Child, David Luan, Dario Amodei, and Ilya Sutskever. 2019. Language models are unsupervised multitask learners. *OpenAI blog*, 1(8):9.

Baptiste Roziere, Marie-Anne Lachaux, Marc Szafraniec, and Guillaume Lample. 2021. Dobf: A deobfuscation pre-training objective for programming languages. *arXiv preprint arXiv:2102.07492*.

Richard Shin, Christopher H. Lin, Sam Thomson, Charles Chen, Subhro Roy, Emmanouil Antonios Platanios, Adam Pauls, Dan Klein, Jason Eisner, and Benjamin Van Durme. 2021. Constrained language models yield few-shot semantic parsers.

Alane Suhr, Srinivasan Iyer, and Yoav Artzi. 2018. Learning to map context-dependent sentences to executable formal queries. In *Proceedings of the 2018 Conference of the North American Chapter of the Association for Computational Linguistics: Human Language Technologies, Volume 1 (Long Papers)*, pages 2238–2249, New Orleans, Louisiana. Association for Computational Linguistics.

Zeyu Sun, Qihao Zhu, Yingfei Xiong, Yican Sun, Lili Mou, and Lu Zhang. 2019. Treegen: A tree-based transformer architecture for code generation. *CoRR*, abs/1911.09983.

Jeniya Tabassum, Mounica Maddela, Wei Xu, and Alan Ritter. 2020. Code and named entity recognition in StackOverflow. In *Proceedings of the 58th Annual Meeting of the Association for Computational Linguistics*, pages 4913–4926, Online. Association for Computational Linguistics.

Ashish Vaswani, Noam Shazeer, Niki Parmar, Jakob Uszkoreit, Llion Jones, Aidan N Gomez, Lukasz Kaiser, and Illia Polosukhin. 2017. Attention is all you need. *arXiv preprint arXiv:1706.03762*.

Thomas Wolf, Lysandre Debut, Victor Sanh, Julien Chaumond, Clement Delangue, Anthony Moi, Pierric Cistac, Tim Rault, Remi Louf, Morgan Funtowicz, Joe Davison, Sam Shleifer, Patrick von Platen, Clara Ma, Yacine Jernite, Julien Plu, Canwen Xu, Teven Le Scao, Sylvain Gugger, Mariama Drame, Quentin Lhoest, and Alexander Rush. 2020. Transformers: State-of-the-art natural language processing. In *Proceedings of the 2020 Conference on Empirical Methods in Natural Language Processing: System Demonstrations*, pages 38–45, Online. Association for Computational Linguistics.

Chunyang Xiao, Marc Dymetman, and Claire Gardent. 2016. Sequence-based structured prediction for semantic parsing. In *Proceedings of the 54th Annual Meeting of the Association for Computational Linguistics (Volume 1: Long Papers)*, pages 1341–1350, Berlin, Germany. Association for Computational Linguistics.

Frank F. Xu, Zhengbao Jiang, Pengcheng Yin, Bogdan Vasilescu, and Graham Neubig. 2020. Incorporating external knowledge through pre-training for natural language to code generation. In *Proceedings of the 58th Annual Meeting of the Association for Computational Linguistics*, pages 6045–6052, Online. Association for Computational Linguistics.

Frank F Xu, Bogdan Vasilescu, and Graham Neubig. 2021. In-ide code generation from natural language: Promise and challenges. *arXiv preprint arXiv:2101.11149*.

Ziyu Yao, Daniel S. Weld, Wei-Peng Chen, and Huan Sun. 2018. Staqc: A systematically mined question-code dataset from stack overflow. In *Proceedings of the 2018 World Wide Web Conference*, WWW '18, page 1693–1703, Republic and Canton of Geneva, CHE. International World Wide Web Conferences Steering Committee.

Pengcheng Yin, Bowen Deng, Edgar Chen, Bogdan Vasilescu, and Graham Neubig. 2018. Learning to mine aligned code and natural language pairs from stack overflow. In *2018 IEEE/ACM 15th International Conference on Mining Software Repositories (MSR)*, pages 476–486. IEEE.

Pengcheng Yin and Graham Neubig. 2017. A syntactic neural model for general-purpose code generation. In *Proceedings of the 55th Annual Meeting of the Association for Computational Linguistics (Volume 1: Long Papers)*, pages 440–450, Vancouver, Canada. Association for Computational Linguistics.

Pengcheng Yin and Graham Neubig. 2018. TRANX: A transition-based neural abstract syntax parser for semantic parsing and code generation. In *Proceedings of the 2018 Conference on Empirical Methods in Natural Language Processing: System Demonstrations*, pages 7–12, Brussels, Belgium. Association for Computational Linguistics.

Pengcheng Yin and Graham Neubig. 2019. Reranking for neural semantic parsing. In *Proceedings of the 57th Annual Meeting of the Association for Computational Linguistics*, pages 4553–4559, Florence, Italy. Association for Computational Linguistics.

Tao Yu, Rui Zhang, Kai Yang, Michihiro Yasunaga, Dongxu Wang, Zifan Li, James Ma, Irene Li, Qingning Yao, Shanelle Roman, Zilin Zhang, and Dragomir Radev. 2018. Spider: A large-scale human-labeled dataset for complex and cross-domain semantic parsing and text-to-SQL task. In *Proceedings of the 2018 Conference on Empirical Methods in Natural Language Processing*, pages 3911–3921, Brussels, Belgium. Association for Computational Linguistics.

John M. Zelle and Raymond J. Mooney. 1996. Learning to parse database queries using inductive logic programming. In *Proceedings of the Thirteenth National Conference on Artificial Intelligence - Volume 2*, AAAI'96, page 1050–1055. AAAI Press.

Luke S. Zettlemoyer and Michael Collins. 2005. Learning to map sentences to logical form: Structured classification with probabilistic categorial grammars. In *Proceedings of the Twenty-First Conference on Uncertainty in Artificial Intelligence*, UAI'05, page 658–666, Arlington, Virginia, USA. AUAI Press.

A Error Categories

	Error Count	General Invalid Syntax	Paranthesis Matching	Other Matching
Baseline	61	39.34	45.90	14.75
+Mined	38	47.37	39.47	13.16
Body	104	39.42	46.15	14.42
-Code	82	30.49	60.98	8.54
-NL	75	25.33	53.33	21.33
-Blocks	94	36.17	53.19	10.64
-Inline	85	28.24	61.18	10.59
Body+Mined	59	38.98	49.15	11.86
-Code	52	26.92	67.31	5.77
-NL	48	33.33	47.92	18.75
-Blocks	51	23.53	66.67	9.80
-Inline	51	41.18	54.90	3.92

Table 8: Percentages of syntax errors for ablations in a single run.

	No Print	Has Print in Snippet	Has Print in Body	Has Print in Both
Baseline	88.28	84.62	86.59	84.21
+Mined	92.97	100.00	91.46	78.95
Body	78.91	84.62	82.93	63.16
-Code	84.38	92.31	80.49	73.68
-NL	84.38	84.62	89.02	78.95
-Blocks	82.29	92.31	76.83	68.42
-Inline	83.07	76.92	86.59	68.42
Body+Mined	90.89	92.31	81.71	57.89
-Code	91.67	69.23	84.15	84.21
-NL	89.84	100.00	91.46	89.47
-Blocks	90.36	92.31	92.68	63.16
-Inline	90.89	92.31	87.80	73.68

Table 9: Percentage of valid snippets based on the presence of `print`.

B Full Questions for Examples

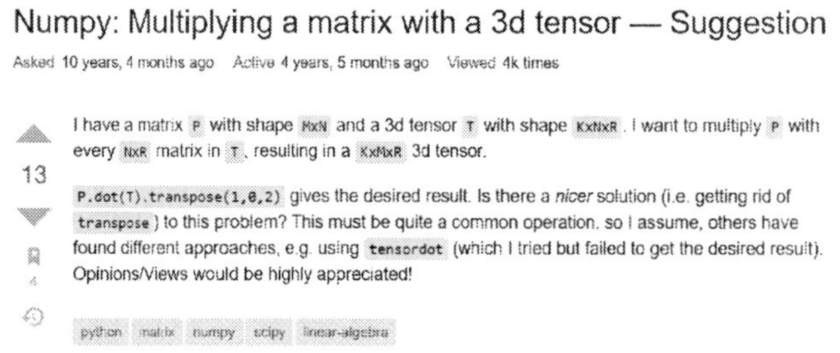

Numpy: Multiplying a matrix with a 3d tensor — Suggestion

Asked 10 years, 4 months ago Active 4 years, 5 months ago Viewed 4k times

13

I have a matrix `P` with shape `MxN` and a 3d tensor `T` with shape `KxNxR`. I want to multiply `P` with every `NxR` matrix in `T`, resulting in a `KxMxR` 3d tensor.

`P.dot(T).transpose(1,0,2)` gives the desired result. Is there a *nicer* solution (i.e. getting rid of `transpose`) to this problem? This must be quite a common operation, so I assume, others have found different approaches, e.g. using `tensordot` (which I tried but failed to get the desired result). Opinions/Views would be highly appreciated!

python matrix numpy scipy linear-algebra

(a) Full Stack Overflow Question for Example 1 in Table 7. Question can be found https://stackoverflow.com/questions/4490961/numpy-multiplying-a-matrix-with-a-3d-tensor-suggestion.

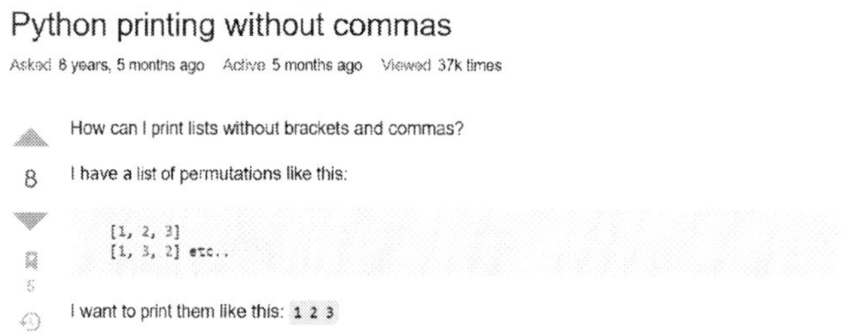

Python printing without commas

Asked 8 years, 5 months ago Active 5 months ago Viewed 37k times

8

How can I print lists without brackets and commas?

I have a list of permutations like this:

```
[1, 2, 3]
[1, 3, 2] etc..
```

I want to print them like this: `1 2 3`

(b) Full Stack Overflow Question for Example 2 in Table 7. Question can be found https://stackoverflow.com/questions/13550423/python-printing-without-commas.

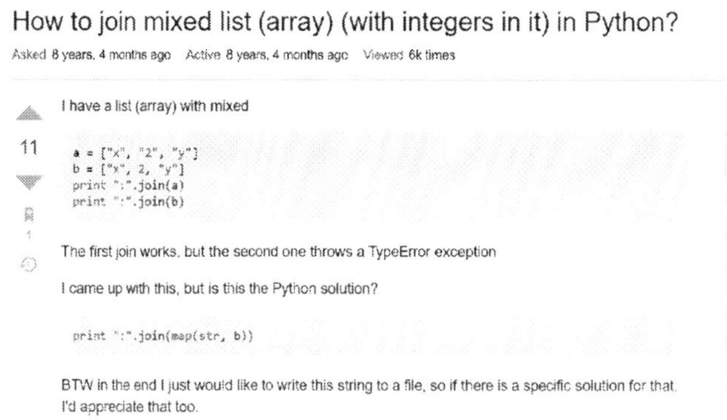

How to join mixed list (array) (with integers in it) in Python?

Asked 8 years, 4 months ago Active 8 years, 4 months ago Viewed 6k times

11

I have a list (array) with mixed

```
a = ["x", "2", "y"]
b = ["x", 2, "y"]
print ":".join(a)
print ":".join(b)
```

The first join works, but the second one throws a TypeError exception

I came up with this, but is this the Python solution?

```
print ":".join(map(str, b))
```

BTW in the end I just would like to write this string to a file, so if there is a specific solution for that, I'd appreciate that too.

(c) Full Stack Overflow Question for Example 3 in Table 7. Question can be found https://stackoverflow.com/questions/13954222/how-to-join-mixed-list-array-with-integers-in-it-in-python.

Text-to-SQL in the Wild: A Naturally-Occurring Dataset Based on Stack Exchange Data

Moshe Hazoom[1] **Vibhor Malik**[2] **Ben Bogin**[1,3]
[1]Rupert [2]Columbia University [3]Tel Aviv University
{ben,moshe}@hirupert.com, malik.vibhor@columbia.edu

Abstract

Most available semantic parsing datasets, comprising of pairs of natural utterances and logical forms, were collected solely for the purpose of training and evaluation of natural language understanding systems. As a result, they do not contain any of the richness and variety of natural-occurring utterances, where humans ask about data they need or are curious about. In this work, we release SEDE, a dataset with 12,023 pairs of utterances and SQL queries collected from real usage on the Stack Exchange website. We show that these pairs contain a variety of real-world challenges which were rarely reflected so far in any other semantic parsing dataset, propose an evaluation metric based on comparison of partial query clauses that is more suitable for real-world queries, and conduct experiments with strong baselines, showing a large gap between the performance on SEDE compared to other common datasets.

Title: *Questions which attract bad answers*
Description: *posts which have attracted significantly more controversial or bad answers than good ones*

```
SELECT p.Id as [Post Link], p.Score from (
 SELECT p.ParentId, count(*) as ContACnt from (
  SELECT PostId,
   up = sum(case when VoteTypeId = 2 then 1
     else 0 end),
   down = sum(case when VoteTypeId = 3 then 1
     else 0 end)
   FROM Votes v join Posts p on p.Id = v.PostId
   WHERE VoteTypeId in (2,3) and PostTypeId = 2
   group by PostId
 ) as ContA
 JOIN posts p on ContA.PostId = p.Id
 WHERE down > (up / ##UVDVRatio:int##) and
 (down + up) > ##MinVotes:int##
 GROUP BY p.ParentId
) as ContQ
JOIN posts p on ContQ.ParentId = p.Id
WHERE ContQ.ContACnt > (p.AnswerCount / 2) and
p.AnswerCount > 1
ORDER BY Score desc
```

Table 1: Example from SEDE for a title and description given by the user, together with the SQL query that the user has written.

1 Introduction

Semantic parsing, the task of mapping natural language into logical forms that can be executed on a database or knowledge graph, has been studied mostly on *academic datasets*, where both the utterances and the queries were written as part of a dataset collection process (Hemphill et al., 1990; Zelle and Mooney, 1996; Yu et al., 2018), and not in a natural process where users ask questions about data they need or are curious about. As a result, these datasets generally do not contain any of the richness and diversity of natural-occurring utterances, even if the data on which the questions are asked about is collected from a real-world source.

Recent methods (Wang et al., 2020a; Herzig et al., 2020; Yu et al., 2021) have significantly improved results on such academic datasets: state-of-the-art models have yield impressive results of over 70%, for example, on Spider (Yu et al., 2018) in a challenging cross-domain setup, where models are trained and tested on different domains, and up to 80%-90% (Nguyen et al., 2021; Zhao and Huang, 2014) on single-domain datasets such as ATIS (Hemphill et al., 1990) and GeoQuery (Zelle and Mooney, 1996). While the cross-domain, zero-shot setup introduces many generalization challenges such as non-explicit mentioning of column names and domain-specific phrases (Suhr et al., 2020; Deng et al., 2020), we argue that even in the easier single-domain setup, it is still unclear how well state-of-the-art models generalize to the challenges that arise from real-world utterances and queries.

In this work, we take a significant step towards evaluation of Text-to-SQL models in a real-world setting, by releasing SEDE: a dataset comprised of 12,023 complex and diverse SQL queries and their natural language titles and descriptions, written by

Proceedings of the 1st Workshop on Natural Language Processing for Programming (NLP4Prog 2021), pages 77–87
August 1–6, 2021.

real users of the Stack Exchange Data Explorer out of a natural interaction.

In Table 1 we show an example for a SQL query from SEDE, with its title and description. It introduces several challenges that have not been commonly addressed in currently available datasets: comparison between different subsets, complex usage of 2 nested sub-queries and an under-specified question, which doesn't state what *"significantly more"* means (solved in this case with an input parameter, `##UVDVRation##`).

Compared to other Text-to-SQL datasets, we show that SEDE contains at least 10 times more SQL queries templates (queries after canonization and anonymization of values) than other datasets, and has the most diverse set of utterances and SQL queries (in terms of 3-grams) out of all single-domain datasets. We manually analyze a sample of examples from the dataset and list the introduced challenges, such as under-specification, usage of parameters in queries, dates manipulation and more.

We also address the challenging problem of evaluating naturally-occurring Text-to-SQL datasets. In academic datasets, standard evaluation metrics such as denotation accuracy and exact comparison of SQL components can often be used with relative success, but we found this to be a greater challenge in SEDE. Denotation accuracy is inaccurate for under-specified utterances, where any single clause not mentioned in the question could entirely change execution results, while exact match comparison of SQL components (e.g. comparing all `SELECT`, `WHERE`, `GROUP BY` and `ORDER BY` clauses) are often too strict when queries are highly complex. While solving these issues still remains an open problem, to at least partially address them we propose to measure a softer version of the exact match metric, PCM-F1, based on partially extracted queries components, and show that this metric gives a better indication of models' performance than common metrics, which yield a score that is close to 0.

Finally, we test strong baselines on our dataset, and show that even models that get strong results on Spider's development set (63.2% Exact-Match, 86.3% PCM-F1), perform poorly on our dataset, with a PCM-F1 value of 50.6%. We hope that the unique and challenging properties exhibited in SEDE[1] will pave a path for future work on generalization of Text-to-SQL models in real world setups.

2 Background

In the past decades, a broad selection of datasets have been used as benchmarks for semantic parsing: ATIS (Hemphill et al., 1990), GeoQuery (Zelle and Mooney, 1996), Restaurants (Tang and Mooney, 2000), Scholar (Iyer et al., 2017), Academic (Li and Jagadish, 2014), Yelp and IMDB (Yaghmazadeh et al., 2017), Advising (Finegan-Dollak et al., 2018), WikiSQL (Zhong et al., 2017), Spider (Yu et al., 2018), WikiTableQuestions (Pasupat and Liang, 2015), Overnight (Wang et al., 2015) and more. However, the utterances and queries in all of these academic datasets, to the best of our knowledge, were collected explicitly for the purpose of evaluating semantic parsing models, usually with the help of crowd-sourcing (even though in most cases questions are asked about real data). As such, these academic datasets were generated in an artificial process, which often introduces various simplifications and artifacts which are not seen in real-life.

Utterance-Query alignment One arising issue with this artificial process is that utterances are often aligned to their SQL queries counterparts, such that the columns and the required computations are explicitly mentioned (Suhr et al., 2020; Deng et al., 2020). In contrast, natural utterances often do not explicitly mention these, since the schema of the database is not necessarily known to the asking user (for example, the question from Spider "titles of films that include 'Deleted Scenes' in their special feature section" might have been more naturally phrased as "films with deleted scenes" in a real-world setting).

Well-specified utterances Furthermore, the utterances in academic datasets are mostly well-specified, whereas in contrast, natural utterances are often under-specified or ambiguous; they could be interpreted in different ways and in turn be mapped to different SQL queries. Consider the example in Table 1: the definition of *"bad answers"* is not well-defined, and in fact could be subjective. Since under-specified utterances, by definition, can not always be answered correctly, any human or machine attempting to answer such a question would have to either make an assumption

[1] Our dataset and code to run all experiments and metrics is available at `https://github.com/hirupert/sede`.

on the requirement (usually based on previously seen examples) or ask follow-up questions in an interactive setting (Yao et al., 2019; Elgohary et al., 2020, 2021).

Scope Last, in academic datasets the utterances are usually written by crowd-sourced workers, asked to provide utterances on various data domains which they do not necessarily need or are interested with. As a result, the utterances and queries are often not very diverse or realistic, are inherently limited in scope, and might not reflect real-world utterances.

3 Stack Exchange Data Explorer

To introduce a realistic Text-to-SQL benchmark, we gather SQL queries together with their titles and descriptions from a naturally occurring dataset: the Stack Exchange Data Explorer. Stack Exchange is an online question & answers community, with over 3 million questions asked. The Data Explorer[2] allows any user to query the database of Stack Exchange with T-SQL (a SQL variant) to answer any question they are curious about. The database schema[3] is spread across 29 tables and 211 columns. Common utterance topics are published posts, comments, votes, tags, awards, etc.

Any query that users run in the data explorer is logged, and users are able to save the queries with a title and description for future use by the public. All of these logs are available online, and Stack Exchange have agreed to release these queries, together with their title, description and other metadata. We publish our clean version of this log, which contains 12,023 samples, of which a subset of 1,714 examples is verified by humans to be correct and is used for validation and test. In this section, we explain the cleaning process, analyze the characteristics of the dataset and compare it to other semantic parsing datasets.

3.1 Data cleaning

The raw aggregated log contains over 1.6 million queries, however in its raw form many of the rows are duplicated or contain unusable queries or titles. The reason for this large difference between the original data size and the cleaned version is that any time that the author of the query executes it, an entry is saved to the log. This introduces two issues: First, many of the queries are not complete, since they were executed before writing the entire query (these incomplete queries are usually valid and executable, but are missing some expressions with respect to the given title and description). Second, after completing the writing of a correct query, users often keep changing and executing the query, but they do not update the title and description accordingly.

To alleviate these issues, we write rule-based filters that remove bad queries/descriptions pairs with high precision. For example, we filter out examples with numbers in the description, if these numbers do not appear in the query (refer to the preprocessing script in the repository for the complete list of filters and the number of examples each of them filter). Whenever a query has multiple versions due to multiple executions, we take the last executed query which passed all filters. After this filtering step, we are left with 12,309 examples.

Using these filters cleans most of the noise, but not all of it. To complete the cleaning process, we manually go over the examples in the validation and test sets, and either filter-out wrong examples or perform minimal changes to either the utterances or the queries (for example, fix a wrong textual value) to ensure that models are evaluated with correct data. Out of the 2,000 examples that we have evaluated, we have kept 1,024 and fixed 690[4], leading to a total of 1,714 validated examples which we use for validation and test. While we do not perform verification on the training set, the verification procedure on the validation set allows us to estimate that most of the queries (85.7%) are either entirely accurate or need just a minimal change to be entirely accurate. For example, when the utterance is "users in Brazil" while the matching query contains the expression: `WHERE users.location like %russia%` we either change the utterance to "users in russia" or change the expression to `WHERE users.location like %Brazil%`. The final number of all training, validation and test examples is 12,023.

3.2 Dataset Characteristics

In this sub-section, we quantify and analyze the introduced challenges in SEDE, compared to other commonly used semantic parsing datasets.

First, we manually analyze a sample of 100 ex-

[2]Publicly available at `https://data.stackexchange.com/`

[3]`https://tinyurl.com/sedeschema`

[4]We publish both the original and the fixed examples

Category	Dataset			Example test cases	
	SEDE	Spider	ATIS	Title	SQL query
Under specification and Hidden assumptions	87	14	15	*User List: Highest downvotes per day ratio with minimum downvotes*	`WHERE id <> -1`
Parameters	40	0	0	*Rollbacks by a certain user*	`WHERE UserId = @UserId`
Window functions	8	0	0	*List of users in the Philippines.*	`DENSE_RANK() OVER (ORDER BY Reputation DESC)`
Dates manipulation	15	0	0	*Quickest new contributor answers to new contributor questions*	`DATEDIFF(s, Q.CreationDate, A.CreationDate)`
Numerical computations and text manipulation	35	0	0	*Average Number of Views per Tag*	`sum(p.ViewCount)/count(*)`
DECLARE/WITH	11	0	0	*Rollbacks by a certain user*	`DECLARE @UserId AS int = ##UserId:int##`
CASE	10	0	0	*Questions and answers per year*	`CASE WHEN Score < 0 THEN 1 ELSE 0 END`

Table 2: Dataset characteristics comparison of randomly selected 100 samples among SEDE and other popular Text-to-SQL datasets.

amples from SEDE and define 7 categories of introduced challenges. To quantify how often each of these concepts appear in SEDE in comparison to other datasets (SPIDER and ATIS), we sample a subset of equal size from each of the other datasets and count the appearances of these concepts. The analysis is shown in Table 2. Next, we describe each of these concepts.

Under specification and Hidden assumptions Utterances in SEDE are often under-specified, that is, they could be interpreted in different ways. For example, when users write *"top users"*, they might refer to users with the most reputation, but also to users that have written the most answers. Likewise, when users write *"last 500 posts"* they might expect to get just the title field of the posts, but possibly also IDs and dates. Similarly, query authors often add various *assumptions* to the queries which are not mentioned in the questions, because they require some knowledge of the available data. For example, they might filter out a special "Community" user in StackExchange, which should not be accounted for in computation of votes. We consider an utterance/query pair to be under-specified or contain an hidden assumption whenever the query contains an expression in any of the SQL clauses (`SELECT`, `WHERE`, etc.) which is *not* specified in the utterance, or where it is specified in an ambiguous way.

Parameters In some cases, query authors can address under-specified utterances by letting the user fill in the under-specified parameters, which are marked in SEDE with either two hashtags (#) on each side of the parameter name, optionally including the required value type (int, string, etc.) and a default value (e.g. `##UserId:int##`), or using a declared variable using SQL syntax (e.g. `@UserId`). For example, in Table 1, the parameter `##UVDVRatio:int##` is used to indicate that the user should fill in an integer to specify the ratio that *"significantly more"* refers to. More broadly, parameters are also helpful for re-usability, allowing users unfamiliar with a query to effortlessly change some values in it.

Window functions Window functions operate on a set of rows and return a single value for each row from the underlying query, thus allowing to perform various aggregation operators without the need for a separate aggregation query. Window functions are often used in SEDE to report percentiles of a specific value in a row, by using operators such as `ROW_NUMBER() OVER`, `NTILE`, `TOP(X) PERCENT`, etc.

Dates manipulation Queries in SEDE sometimes contain dates arithmetic expressions. See the example category query in Table 2: this expression calculates the difference in seconds from the time the question was created to the time the answer was created.

Numerical computations and text manipulation Queries can perform any arbitrary numerical computation and text manipulation. The computations in SEDE often include multiple nested operators including rounding and conversions to float, for example: `ROUND(CAST(Main.Total AS FLOAT) / Meta.Total, 2) AS 'Ratio'`. Queries can also contain text manipulation such as concatenation, for example: `'stackoverflow.com/tags/' + t.tagName + '/info' as [Link]` which builds a URL from a tag name.

Dataset	Unique Utterances	Unique Queries	Average unique Tables / uttr	Utterance 3-gram	SQL 3-gram	Avg. nesting Level	Unique Templates	Average unique Queries / template
Spider	8,034	4491	1.71	41.7K	25.2K	1.15	1,059	7.6
WikiSQL	**80,654**†	**77,840**†	1†	**375K**	**209K**	1†	488†	165.3†
Academic	196†	185†	3.0†	<1K	<1K	1.04†	92†	2.1†
Advising	4,570†	211†	3.0†	20K	11.2K	1.18†	174†	20.3†
ATIS	5,280†	947†	**3.8**†	13.2K	5.8K	1.39†	751†	7.0†
GeoQuery	877†	246†	1.1†	1.5K	1.4K	**2.03**†	98†	8.9†
IMDB	131†	89†	1.9†	<1K	<1K	1.01†	52†	2.5†
Restaurants	378†	23†	2.3†	<1K	<1K	1.17†	17†	22.2†
Scholar	817†	193†	3.2†	2.6K	2.2K	1.02†	146†	5.6†
Yelp	128†	110†	1.0†	<1K	<1K	1.0†	89†	1.4†
SEDE	12,023	11,767	2.14	42.6K	173K	1.28	**10,664**	**1.1**

Table 3: Comparison of different semantic parsing datasets (for Spider, analysis is performed on training and validation sets only). † denotes that numbers are reported from Finegan-Dollak et al. (2018). Average Unique Queries / template denotes the number of different SQL queries per template, thus lower means more diversity in the dataset. Datasets above dashed line are cross-domain, and below it are single-domain.

DECLARE/WITH SQL queries can be written as a procedural process, where multiple commands are executed sequentially. Query authors can store values in simple variables with `DECLARE`, but more importantly, they can store complete "views" of tables with the `WITH` command. While these commands do not add any expressivity (that is, any query can be written without these commands), they allow writing more clear and concise queries with less nested expressions.

CASE The `CASE` clause is similar to an *if-then-else* statement of any programming language, and is often used to either make the query more readable (e.g. by returning names of values instead of integers) or to perform conditional logic. For example, the clause in Table 2 (last row) counts negative scores using `CASE` function.

Comparison In Table 2 we see that a vast majority of SEDE is not well-specified, which implies that in order for Text-to-SQL models to work robustly in a real-world setting, it should identify cases of ambiguity and possibly proceed with follow-up questions. We see that the rest of the concepts appear in 10% to 40% of SEDE examples, whereas these concepts are not exhibited in any other analyzed dataset.

Next, we show a comparison of quantifiable metrics of popular Text-to-SQL datasets compared to SEDE in Table 3. We see that SEDE is the largest dataset in terms of unique utterances and queries out of all single-domain datasets. To compare diversity and scope, we also measure the number of unique 3-grams for both the utterances and the queries, and see that SEDE has a very diverse set of SQL 3-grams, with almost 6 times the number of the next follower, Spider, and only 17% less than WikiSQL, which is 6.6 bigger in terms of queries. The number of utterance 3-gram is the second largest, after WikiSQL. Last, we count the number of unique *SQL templates*, as defined in Finegan-Dollak et al. (2018): we anonymize the values and group all canonized queries. We see that SEDE has more than 10 times templates than the follower Spider, and that the average number of queries per template is the lowest. We also see that SEDE is third in terms of average nesting level, after ATIS and GeoQuery.

3.3 Limitations

We note that in order to simulate the most realistic setting, an ideal Text-to-SQL dataset would include questions asked by users which are completely unaware of the schema, which are not SQL-savy, and that the person asking the question would be different than the person answering it. While this is not the case in SEDE, we believe its setting is still significantly more realistic that other datasets.

4 Evaluation

Semantic parsing models are usually evaluated in two different forms: execution accuracy and logical forms accuracy. In this section, we show why using any of these metrics is difficult with complex queries such as those in SEDE, and propose a more loose metric for evaluation of models.

Execution accuracy This metric is measured by executing both the predicted and gold query against a dataset, and considers the query to be correct if the two output results are the same (or similar enough). While this metric appears to be exactly what we want to optimize (yielding a query the outputs a correct output), it does not necessarily cope well with two challenges: spurious queries and under-specified questions. Spurious queries are incorrect queries (with respect to the given question) that happen to result in a correct answer, thus leading to a false-positive count. The problem of spuriousness can be addressed by executing the predicted query on modified versions of the dataset, as proposed in Zhong et al. (2020). The second challenge, evaluating under-specification, is arguably harder to address, as mentioned in Subsection 3.2. For example, consider a question that asks for *"the top 1% active users"*. This question does not specify which columns should be returned, how the rows should be ordered, and how does one measure "being active". As such, a query could be correct with respect to some interpretation, yet its execution result might be different than the execution result of the given gold query.

Logical form accuracy Instead of comparing execution results, another frequent approach is to simply perform a textual comparison between the predicted and gold queries. When comparing SQL queries, it is common to perform a more loose comparison that does not consider the order of appearances of different clauses (e.g. it shouldn't matter which `WHERE` expression is written first), as performed in Spider (Yu et al., 2018). However, as discussed in Zhong et al. (2020), even this looser metric leads to false-negative measures, since multiple queries can all be correct with respect to an utterance, but written in various different manners. Due to the richness of SQL queries in SEDE, its extended scope and the fact that queries are written by many different authors, in our case this problem deteriorates: queries can be written in a substantial number of ways. For example, a query that contains a `WITH` statement could yield exactly the same result without it, by including a nested `FROM` clause instead.

4.1 Sub-tree elements matching

In this work, in order to alleviate the aforementioned issues with exact-match logical form evaluation, we loosen it so that models can get partial scores if at least some part of their predicted expressions are found in the gold query. We do this by parsing both the predicted query and the gold query, comparing different parts of the two parsed trees and aggregating the scores into a single metric, as defined next. We term this metric **P**artial **C**omponent **M**atch **F1** (PCM-F1).

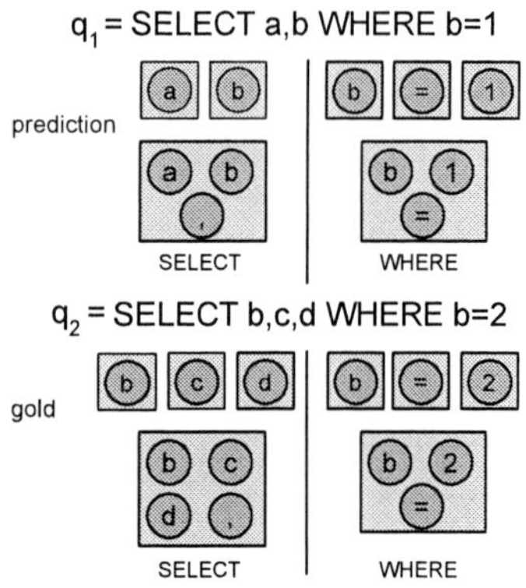

Figure 1: An example for sub-tree matching.

Our proposed metric is based on the "Component Matching" metric which is used in Spider's evaluation (Yu et al., 2019), except that we use a parser that supports a large variety of queries (Spider's parser only supports specific types of queries), define how to compute the metric in a general way (not specific to any SQL-specific clause) and aggregate (average) the F1 scores into a single value, as defined next.

We first use an open-source SQL parser, JSqlParser,[5] to parse a given SQL query q into a tree, and extract a set of elements for each of its sub-trees, considering a sub-tree only if all of its leaves are terminal values in the query (similar to extracting constituents from a parse tree). For example, as can be seen in Figure 1, the predicted query q_1 has 7 relevant sub-trees (marked in rectangles). The sub-tree which represents the expression `b=1` contains four elements: `b`, `=`, `1` and `b=1`. We then split these sets into different categories, based on the SQL query part that the root of the original sub-tree belonged to, for each of the following categories: $C = \{$`SELECT`, `TOP`, `FROM`, `WHERE`, `GROUPBY`, `HAVING`, `ORDERBY`$\}$. We denote all sets of elements for a query q in a category $c \in C$ as $s_c(q)$. For example, as can be seen in Figure 1, the clause $s_{\texttt{SELECT}}(q_1)$ yields 3 sub-trees. Given a predicted query q_p and a gold query q_g, we compute the average F1 metric of all aligned pairs of sets $s_c(q_p)$ and $s_c(q_g)$:

$$\text{PCM-F1}(q_p, q_g) = \frac{1}{\mid C \mid} \sum_{c \in C} F1\left(s_c(q_p), s_c(q_g)\right)$$

[5] https://github.com/JSQLParser/JSqlParser

Model	Spider-Dev				
	PCM-F1	PCM-EM	PCM-F1-NoValues	PCM-EM-NoValues	EM
RAT (Wang et al., 2020b)	88.1	37.3	91.3	69.0	69.7†
RAT+GAP (Shi et al., 2020)	89.3	39.0	92.6	71.8	71.8†
T5-Base *with schema*	85.7	56.7	85.9	57.2	57.6
T5-Large *with schema*	**86.3**	**61.2**	**86.6**	**62.6**	**63.2**

Table 4: Results on Spider with various metrics. While we do not focus on Spider, we show our results for comparison of the model and evaluation metric with a known benchmark. † denotes reported numbers from Spider's official leaderboard. PCM-F1-`NoValues` and PCM-EM-`NoValues` are modified versions of PCM-F1 and PCM-EM, respectively, such that all values in the SQL are anonymized and the `ON` clause is ignored, in order to compare with Spider's official Exact-Match (EM) metric.

where F1 score is the harmonic mean of the precision and recall of the predicted sub-trees $s_c(q_p)$ with respect to the gold sub-trees $s_c(q_g)$. If for some category c, we get that $s_c(q_p)$ is an empty set but $s_c(q_g)$ is not, or vice-versa, we set $F1 = 0.0$ for that category.

Consider Figure 1 for an example. $s_{\texttt{SELECT}}(q_1)$ has 3 sub-trees while the gold category $s_{\texttt{SELECT}}(q_2)$ has 4 sub-trees. The predicted `SELECT` clause has 2 wrong sub-trees (`a` and `a,b`) leading to a precision $p = \frac{1}{3}$, and 2 missing elements leading to a recall $r = \frac{1}{4}$. Similarly, the `WHERE` clause gets a precision of $p = \frac{1}{2}$ and a recall of $r = \frac{1}{2}$. Thus, we get $F1 = 0.285$ for `SELECT` and $F1 = 0.5$ for `WHERE`, leading to a final score PCM-F1 $= 0.392$.

4.2 Limitations

Parsing Queries JSqlParser could only parse 93.2% of the validation SQL queries in SEDE, and 92.5% of the test queries. For that reason, for evaluation we only use the subset of queries which we can parse and evaluate [6]. During evaluation, if the predicted query was not parsed, it receives a score of 0. Note that this does not affect training.

False negatives We note that our metric does not address at all the issue of false negatives - in fact, since it's a looser metric than the Exact Match metric, it is actually more prone to produce false negative outcomes. For SEDE, this issue could be mitigated by improving the similarity function that compares two queries, or by adapting the execution accuracy method in a way that will be less sensitive to instances of under-specification. We leave this challenge for future work.

[6] While we did not use the rest of the validation queries, we have released them in the dataset for future use, assuming at least some of them are valid queries.

Model	SEDE-Dev		SEDE-Test	
	PCM-F1	PCM-EM	PCM-F1	PCM-EM
T5-Base	46.8	**4.0**	49.4	3.6
with schema	46.4	3.4	48.9	**4.5**
T5-Large	**48.2**	**4.0**	50.6	4.1
with schema	47.1	3.7	**51.0**	3.3

Table 5: Results on SEDE development and test sets.

5 Experiments

In this section, we describe our experimental setup, test how strong baselines perform on SEDE, and analyze their errors.

5.1 Experimantal Setup

Most models in the Spider leaderboard[7] use a grammar-based decoder designed for Spider, and as a result, they cannot be used as-is on SEDE, which uses a larger grammar. Thus, following Shaw et al. (2020), we use a general-purpose pre-trained sequence-to-sequence model, T5 (Raffel et al., 2020), which was shown to be competitive with Spider's state-of-the-art models.

Since all queries in SEDE come from a single schema which is seen during training time, it is not clear if allowing the model to access the schema during encoding and decoding is helpful. We thus experiment with two versions. In the first one, T5, the input is simply the utterance $\bar{u}$. In the second, T5 *with schema*, the input is the utterance $\bar{u}$ followed by a separator token, and then the serialized schema. We follow Suhr et al. (2020) and serialize the schema by listing all tables in the schema and all the columns for each table, with a separator token between each column and table. Naturally, we did not evaluate T5 (without schema) on Spider since encoding the schema is crucial in a zero-shot

[7] `https://yale-lily.github.io/spider`

Category & Utterance	Gold	Predicted

Under-specification and Hidden assumptions
 	
Positive scored questions without answers for c++ tags
	SELECT id as "" Post Link "", *
	FROM posts
	WHERE
	  answercount = 0
	  AND tags NOT LIKE '%c++%'
	  AND score > 0
	  AND ClosedDate is null
	ORDER BY score DESC
		SELECT id as [Post Link], tags,
		  score, viewcount, CreationDate
		FROM posts
		WHERE
		  tags NOT LIKE '%c++%'
		  AND answercount = 0
		  AND posttypeid = 1
		  AND score > 0
		  AND CreationDate > '2018-01-01'
		ORDER BY CreationDate DESC

Dates Manipulation
 	
Percentage of votes - depending on day after posting (only questions)
	SELECT
	  DATEDIFF(day, p.CreationDate,
	    v.CreationDate) AS Days,
	  COUNT(v.Id) AS Count,
	  COUNT(v.Id) * 100.0
	    / SUM(COUNT(v.Id)) OVER ()
	    AS Percentage ...
		SELECT
		  DATEDIFF(day, p.CreationDate,
		    v.CreationDate) AS Days,
		  COUNT(v.Id) AS Count,
		  COUNT(v.Id) * 100.0
		    / COUNT(v.Id)
		    AS Percentage ...

Parameters
 	
Top users in a tag by score and answer count
	SELECT TOP 100 ...
	WHERE ...
	  AND t.TagName = 'tagName'
		SELECT TOP ##num?100## Users.id
		  AS [User Link], ...
		WHERE tags.TagName = '##tagname##'

Table 6: Error analysis of gold queries vs. predicted queries for some selected dataset characteristics mentioned in 3. For brevity, in some of the examples we show only relevant parts of the query.

setup. We perform textual pre-processing to the queries in SEDE before training (i.e. remove non UTF-8 characters and SQL comments, normalize spaces and new lines, normalize apostrophes, remove comments, etc.). We show results for experiments considering the titles alone, and ignore their given description, which are given in 14.6% of the examples. We have found that if we concatenate the description to the title, we get slightly worse results.

We use the SentencePiece (Kudo and Richardson, 2018) tokenizer, with its default vocabulary, for all models. We fine-tune the model to minimize the token-level cross-entropy loss against the gold SQL query for 60 epochs with the AdamW (Loshchilov and Hutter, 2019) optimizer and a learning rate of $5e^{-5}$. We choose the best model based on the performance on the validation set for each dataset, using Exact-Match (EM) for Spider and PCM-F1 for SEDE. For inference, we use beam-search (of size 6) and choose the highest-probability generated SQL query. We show results for both T5-Base and T5-Large.

For each experiment we measure PCM-F1 together with a modified version of it, PCM-EM (PCM exact match), that returns an accuracy of 1 for a given prediction if and only if the PCM-F1 value for that prediction is 1. For Spider, we use the officially provided script to measure the EM metric.

5.2 Main Results

We show experiments results for SEDE in Table 5 and for Spider in Table 4. The results indicate that the performance gap between SEDE and Spider is large: while T5-Large reaches a score of 63.2 EM on Spider's validation set, not very far from the state-of-the-art (a difference of 8.6 points), and a PCM-F1 of 86.3, when trained on SEDE, it only receives 48.2 and 50.6 PCM-F1 on the validation and test set of SEDE, respectively. This supports our main claim, that single-schema datasets could still impose a substantial challenge when tested in a realistic setup. We also notice in Table 4 that large improvements in EM do not necessarily imply a large increase in PCM-F1, since PCM-F1 numbers are already high for Spider in any of the tested models, implying that the model is generating SQL queries that are close to the exact gold SQL, only different by a small change (e.g. value or column name).

Comparing experiments with and without encoding the schema shows that encoding the schema does not significantly improve results in this single-domain setup. We also observe that PCM-EM is close to 0 in all experiments, supporting our motivation to create a loosened evaluation metric.

5.3 PCM-F1 Validation

In order to validate the correctness of our proposed evaluation metric, we compare PCM-EM with the more established EM metric of Spider. There are two differences in the way EM is calculated compared to PCM-EM: (1) EM anonymizes all values in the queries and (2) EM ignores the `ON` expressions in the `JOIN` clauses. For those reasons, we define PCM-F1-NoValues and PCM-EM-NoValues, modified versions of PCM-F1 and PCM-EM, respectively, such that all values in the SQL are anonymized and the `ON` expressions are ignored. Table 4 shows that EM and PCM-EM-NoValues are only different by up to 0.7 points for all models, showing that PCM-F1 is well calibrated with Spider's EM.

5.4 Error Analysis

Next, we analyze errors and successful outputs of the model. Table 6 shows examples of gold vs. predicted queries by our model, with respect to some of the introduced challenges mentioned in 3.2.

We can see from the first example that the model is often wrong whenever the question is not specified well: In this example, this happens in the `SELECT`, `WHERE` and `ORDER` fields. In the `SELECT` clause, the model predicts extra columns in comparison to the gold query, most likely as it has learned to do so for similar questions. In addition, since the desired order of the results are not mentioned in the utterance, it leads to a different predicted `ORDER BY` clause. A hidden assumption the author had added to the query is taking into account only open questions (i.e. questions with no close date: `ClosedDate is null`). The model, which could not deduce this assumption from the utterance alone, predicts a wrong filter expression `CreationDate > '2018-01-01'`.

The second example shows how the model correctly uses the `DATEDIFF` function to manipulate dates, although it predicted a wrong computation of the percentage (i.e. without the `SUM` function).

The last example shows how the model generates a SQL query with parameters, for the number of required users (with a predicted default value of 100) and for the tag name. In this case, the predicted query is possibly better than the gold one as it uses a reusable parameter instead of a fixed one.

6 Conclusion

In this work, we take a significant step towards improving and evaluating Text-to-SQL models in a real world setting, by releasing SEDE, a dataset comprised of real-world complex and diverse SQL queries with their utterances, naturally written by real users. We show that there's a large gap between the performance of strong Text-to-SQL baselines on SEDE compared to the commonly studied dataset Spider, and hope that the release of this challenging dataset will encourage research on improving generalization for real-world SQL prediction.

Acknowledgments We thank Kevin Montrose and the rest of the Stack Exchange team for providing the raw query log.

References

Xiang Deng, Ahmed Hassan Awadallah, Chris Meek, Alex Polozov, Huan Sun, and Matthew Richardson. 2020. Structure-grounded pretraining for text-to-sql. Technical Report 2010.12773, Arxiv.

Ahmed Elgohary, Saghar Hosseini, and Ahmed Hassan Awadallah. 2020. Speak to your parser: Interactive text-to-sql with natural language feedback.

Ahmed Elgohary, Christopher Meek, Matthew Richardson, Adam Fourney, Gonzalo Ramos, and Ahmed Hassan Awadallah. 2021. NL-EDIT: Correcting semantic parse errors through natural language interaction. In *Proceedings of the 2021 Conference of the North American Chapter of the Association for Computational Linguistics: Human Language Technologies*, pages 5599–5610, Online. Association for Computational Linguistics.

Catherine Finegan-Dollak, Jonathan K. Kummerfeld, Li Zhang, Karthik Ramanathan, Sesh Sadasivam, Rui Zhang, and Dragomir Radev. 2018. Improving text-to-SQL evaluation methodology. In *Proceedings of the 56th Annual Meeting of the Association for Computational Linguistics (Volume 1: Long Papers)*, pages 351–360, Melbourne, Australia. Association for Computational Linguistics.

Charles T. Hemphill, John J. Godfrey, and George R. Doddington. 1990. The ATIS spoken language systems pilot corpus. In *Speech and Natural Language: Proceedings of a Workshop Held at Hidden Valley, Pennsylvania, June 24-27,1990.*

Jonathan Herzig, Pawel Krzysztof Nowak, Thomas Müller, Francesco Piccinno, and Julian Eisenschlos. 2020. TaPas: Weakly supervised table parsing via pre-training. In *Proceedings of the 58th Annual Meeting of the Association for Computational Linguistics*, pages 4320–4333, Online. Association for Computational Linguistics.

Srinivasan Iyer, Ioannis Konstas, Alvin Cheung, Jayant Krishnamurthy, and Luke Zettlemoyer. 2017. Learning a neural semantic parser from user feedback. *CoRR*, abs/1704.08760.

Taku Kudo and John Richardson. 2018. SentencePiece: A simple and language independent subword tokenizer and detokenizer for neural text processing. In *Proceedings of the 2018 Conference on Empirical Methods in Natural Language Processing: System Demonstrations*, pages 66–71, Brussels, Belgium. Association for Computational Linguistics.

Fei Li and H. V. Jagadish. 2014. Constructing an interactive natural language interface for relational databases. *Proc. VLDB Endow.*, 8(1):73–84.

Ilya Loshchilov and Frank Hutter. 2019. Decoupled weight decay regularization.

Phuong Minh Nguyen, Vu Tran, and Minh Le Nguyen. 2021. Phrasetransformer: Self-attention using local context for semantic parsing.

Panupong Pasupat and Percy Liang. 2015. Compositional semantic parsing on semi-structured tables. In *Proceedings of the 53rd Annual Meeting of the Association for Computational Linguistics and the 7th International Joint Conference on Natural Language Processing (Volume 1: Long Papers)*, pages 1470–1480, Beijing, China. Association for Computational Linguistics.

Colin Raffel, Noam Shazeer, Adam Roberts, Katherine Lee, Sharan Narang, Michael Matena, Yanqi Zhou, Wei Li, and Peter J. Liu. 2020. Exploring the limits of transfer learning with a unified text-to-text transformer.

Peter Shaw, Ming-Wei Chang, Panupong Pasupat, and Kristina Toutanova. 2020. Compositional generalization and natural language variation: Can a semantic parsing approach handle both?

Peng Shi, Patrick Ng, Zhiguo Wang, Henghui Zhu, Alexander Hanbo Li, Jun Wang, Cicero Nogueira dos Santos, and Bing Xiang. 2020. Learning contextual representations for semantic parsing with generation-augmented pre-training.

Alane Suhr, Ming-Wei Chang, Peter Shaw, and Kenton Lee. 2020. Exploring unexplored generalization challenges for cross-database semantic parsing. In *Proceedings of the 58th Annual Meeting of the Association for Computational Linguistics*, pages 8372–8388, Online. Association for Computational Linguistics.

Lappoon R. Tang and Raymond J. Mooney. 2000. Automated construction of database interfaces: Integrating statistical and relational learning for semantic parsing. EMNLP '00, page 133–141, USA. Association for Computational Linguistics.

Bailin Wang, Richard Shin, Xiaodong Liu, Oleksandr Polozov, and Matthew Richardson. 2020a. RAT-SQL: Relation-aware schema encoding and linking for text-to-SQL parsers. In *Proceedings of the 58th Annual Meeting of the Association for Computational Linguistics*, pages 7567–7578, Online. Association for Computational Linguistics.

Bailin Wang, Richard Shin, Xiaodong Liu, Oleksandr Polozov, and Matthew Richardson. 2020b. Rat-sql: Relation-aware schema encoding and linking for text-to-sql parsers.

Yushi Wang, Jonathan Berant, and Percy Liang. 2015. Building a semantic parser overnight. In *Proceedings of the 53rd Annual Meeting of the Association for Computational Linguistics and the 7th International Joint Conference on Natural Language Processing (Volume 1: Long Papers)*, pages 1332–1342, Beijing, China. Association for Computational Linguistics.

Navid Yaghmazadeh, Yuepeng Wang, Isil Dillig, and Thomas Dillig. 2017. Sqlizer: Query synthesis from natural language. *Proc. ACM Program. Lang.*, 1(OOPSLA).

Ziyu Yao, Yu Su, Huan Sun, and Wen-tau Yih. 2019. Model-based interactive semantic parsing: A unified framework and a text-to-SQL case study. In *Proceedings of the 2019 Conference on Empirical Methods in Natural Language Processing and the 9th International Joint Conference on Natural Language Processing (EMNLP-IJCNLP)*, pages 5447–5458, Hong Kong, China. Association for Computational Linguistics.

Tao Yu, Chien-Sheng Wu, Xi Victoria Lin, bailin wang, Yi Chern Tan, Xinyi Yang, Dragomir Radev, richard socher, and Caiming Xiong. 2021. GraPPa: Grammar-augmented pre-training for table semantic parsing. In *International Conference on Learning Representations*.

Tao Yu, Rui Zhang, Kai Yang, Michihiro Yasunaga, Dongxu Wang, Zifan Li, James Ma, Irene Li, Qingning Yao, Shanelle Roman, Zilin Zhang, and Dragomir Radev. 2018. Spider: A large-scale human-labeled dataset for complex and cross-domain semantic parsing and text-to-SQL task. In *Proceedings of the 2018 Conference on Empirical Methods in Natural Language Processing*, pages 3911–3921, Brussels, Belgium. Association for Computational Linguistics.

Tao Yu, Rui Zhang, Kai Yang, Michihiro Yasunaga, Dongxu Wang, Zifan Li, James Ma, Irene Li, Qingning Yao, Shanelle Roman, Zilin Zhang, and Dragomir Radev. 2019. Spider: A large-scale human-labeled dataset for complex and cross-domain semantic parsing and text-to-sql task.

John M. Zelle and Raymond J. Mooney. 1996. Learning to parse database queries using inductive logic programming. In *Proceedings of the Thirteenth National Conference on Artificial Intelligence - Volume 2*, AAAI'96, page 1050–1055. AAAI Press.

Kai Zhao and Liang Huang. 2014. Type-driven incremental semantic parsing with polymorphism.

Ruiqi Zhong, Tao Yu, and Dan Klein. 2020. Semantic evaluation for text-to-SQL with distilled test suites.

In *Proceedings of the 2020 Conference on Empirical Methods in Natural Language Processing (EMNLP)*, pages 396–411, Online. Association for Computational Linguistics.

Victor Zhong, Caiming Xiong, and Richard Socher. 2017. Seq2sql: Generating structured queries from natural language using reinforcement learning.

Bag-of-Words Baselines for Semantic Code Search

Xinyu Zhang,[1] **Ji Xin,**[1] **Andrew Yates,**[2] and **Jimmy Lin**[1]

[1] David R. Cheriton School of Computer Science, University of Waterloo
[2] Max Planck Institute for Informatics, Saarland Informatics Campus

Abstract

The task of *semantic code search* is to retrieve code snippets from a source code corpus based on an information need expressed in natural language. The semantic gap between natural language and programming languages has for long been regarded as one of the most significant obstacles to the effectiveness of keyword-based information retrieval (IR) methods. It is a common assumption that "traditional" bag-of-words IR methods are poorly suited for semantic code search: our work empirically investigates this assumption. Specifically, we examine the effectiveness of two traditional IR methods, namely BM25 and RM3, on the CodeSearchNet Corpus, which consists of natural language queries paired with relevant code snippets. We find that the two keyword-based methods outperform several pre-BERT neural models. We also compare several code-specific data pre-processing strategies and find that specialized tokenization improves effectiveness. Code for reproducing our experiments is available at `https://github.com/crystina-z/CodeSearchNet-baseline`.

1 Introduction

Community Question Answering forums like Stack Overflow have become popular[1] methods for finding code snippets relevant to natural language questions (e.g., *"How can I download a paper from arXiv in Python?"*). Such forums require community members to provide answers, which means that potential questions are limited to public code, and a large portion of questions cannot be answered in real time. The task of semantic code search removes these limitations by treating a code-related natural language question as a query and using it to retrieve relevant code snippets. In this way, novel questions can be immediately answered whether in public or private code repositories.

Consequently, the semantic code search task is receiving an increasing amount of attention. Several early efforts showed promising results applying neural networks models to various code search datasets (Gu et al., 2018; Sachdev et al., 2018; Cambronero et al., 2019; Zhu et al., 2020; Srinivas et al., 2020). To facilitate research on semantic code search, GitHub released the CodeSearchNet Corpus and Challenge (Husain et al., 2019), providing a large-scale dataset across multiple programming languages with unified evaluation criteria. This dataset has been utilized by multiple recent papers (Feng et al., 2020; Gu et al., 2021; Sun et al., 2020; Arumugam, 2020).

Work on semantic code search has focused on neural ranking models under the assumption that such methods are necessary to bridge the semantic gap between natural language queries and relevant results (i.e., code snippets). Such approaches usually design a task-specific joint vector representation to map natural language queries and programming language "documents" into a shared vector space (Gu et al., 2018; Sachdev et al., 2018; Cambronero et al., 2019). Inspired by progress in pretrained models (Devlin et al., 2019), researchers proposed CodeBERT (Feng et al., 2020), a pretrained transformer model specifically for programming languages, which yields impressive effectiveness on this task.

Beyond utilizing the raw text of code corpora, another thread of research conducts retrieval using structural features parsed from code, which are believed to contain rich semantic information (Srinivas et al., 2020). Multiple papers have also proposed incorporating structural information with neural ranking models (Gu et al., 2021; Sun et al., 2020; Ling et al., 2021; Guo et al., 2020).

[1] `https://stackoverflow.blog/2020/01/21/scripting-the-future-of-stack-2020-plans-vision/`

Proceedings of the 1st Workshop on Natural Language Processing for Programming (NLP4Prog 2021), pages 88–94
August 1–6, 2021. ©2021 Association for Computational Linguistics

In contrast to these comparatively sophisticated methods, in this work we explore the effectiveness of traditional information retrieval (IR) methods on the semantic code search task. This exploration is of interest for two reasons:

First, while neural methods can take advantage of distributed representations (i.e., static or contextual embeddings) to model semantic similarity, Yang et al. (2019) found that pre-BERT neural ranking models can underperform traditional IR methods like BM25 with RM3 query expansion, especially in the absence of large amounts of data for training. Prior work has claimed that traditional IR methods are unfit for code search (Husain et al., 2019), but there is a lack of empirical evidence supporting this claim. In fact, in one of the few comparisons with traditional IR methods available (Sachdev et al., 2018), BM25 performed well in comparison to the proposed neural methods on an Android-specific dataset.

Second, neural approaches are often reranking methods that rerank candidate documents identified by a first-stage ranking method. Even dense retrieval methods that perform ranking on shared vector representations directly can benefit from hybrid combinations with keyword-based signals as well as another round of reranking (Gao et al., 2020). It is thus useful to identify the best-performing traditional IR methods in this domain, so that they can provide a complementary source of evidence.

Thus, our work has two main contributions: First, we provide strong keyword baselines for semantic code search, demonstrating that traditional IR methods can in fact outperform several pre-BERT neural ranking models even without a semantic matching ability, which extends the conclusions drawn by Yang et al. (2019) on *ad hoc* retrieval to the semantic code search task. Second, we investigate and quantify the impact of specialized pre-processing for code search.

2 Related Work

As discussed above, joint-vector representations have been widely used in recent work on code search. NCS (Sachdev et al., 2018) proposed an approach integrating TF-IDF, word embeddings, and an efficient embedding search technique where the word embeddings are learned in an unsupervised manner. CODEnn (Gu et al., 2018) developed a neural model based on queries and separate code components. UNIF (Cambronero et al., 2019) investigated the necessity of supervision and sophisticated architectures for learning aligned vector representations. After concluding that supervision and a simpler network architecture are beneficial, the authors further enhanced NCS by adding a supervision module on top. In addition to introducing the dataset, the CodeSearchNet paper also proposed joint-embedding models as baselines, where the embeddings may be learned from neural bag of words (NBoW), bidirectional RNN, 1D CNN, or self-attention (SelfAtt). In this work, we compare against the best-performing of these baselines, NBoW and SelfAtt.

Unlike attempts to learn aligned vector representations from each dataset, CodeBERT (Feng et al., 2020) built a BERT-style pre-trained transformer encoder with code-specific training data and objectives, and then fine-tuned the model on downstream tasks. This approach has been highly successful.

Another line of work tries to enhance retrieval by incorporating structural information. In work where queries and code snippets are encoded separately, this is usually achieved by merging the encoded structure into the code vector. Sun et al. (2020) extracted paths from the abstract syntax tree (AST) of the code and directly used the encoded path to represent the code snippet. Gu et al. (2021) built a statement dependency matrix from the code and transformed it into a vector, which is then added to the code vector prepared from the text. Ling et al. (2021) utilized a graph neural network to embed the *program graph* into the code vector. Adopting a different approach, Guo et al. (2020) extended CodeBERT by adding two structure-aware pre-training objectives, and showed that the benefits of structural information are orthogonal to the benefits of large-scale pre-training.

While neural ranking models are popular approaches to the code retrieval task, we found few papers that compared them with traditional algorithms. To the best of our knowledge, only Sachdev et al. (2018) compared their embedding model with BM25, finding that BM25 performed acceptably.

3 Models

In this section, we describe the traditional IR methods that we used in our experiments and the neural ranking models that have been evaluated on the CodeSearchNet Corpus in previous work (Husain et al., 2019; Feng et al., 2020).

3.1 Traditional IR Baselines

To test the effectiveness of traditional IR methods, we chose two well-known and effective retrieval methods as our baselines: BM25 (Robertson and Zaragoza, 2009) and RM3 (Lavrenko and Croft, 2001; Abdul-Jaleel et al., 2004). Both have been widely used for *ad hoc* retrieval and have been demonstrated to be strong baselines compared to multiple pre-BERT neural ranking models (Yang et al., 2019).

BM25 is a ranking method based on the probabilistic relevance model (Robertson and Jones, 1976), which combines term frequency (tf) and inverse document frequency (idf) signals from individual query terms to estimate query–document relevance. RM3 is a query expansion technique based on pseudo relevance feedback (PRF) that can be combined with another ranking method such as BM25. It expands the original query with selected terms from initial retrieval results (e.g., results of BM25) and applies another round of retrieval (e.g., with BM25) using the expanded query. We omit a comprehensive explanation of these two methods here and refer interested readers to the cited papers.

3.2 Neural Ranking Models

We compare the traditional IR methods described above with three neural ranking models: neural bag of words (NBoW), self-attention (SelfAtt), and CodeBERT. Results of the first two models are reported by Husain et al. (2019), and the last model by Feng et al. (2020). We use their reported scores in this paper.

According to Husain et al. (2019), both NBoW and SelfAtt encode natural language queries and code into a joint vector space, and then aggregate the sequence representation into a single vector. The models are trained with the objective of maximizing the inner products of the aggregated query vectors and code vectors. The two models only differ in the *encoding* step, where NBoW encodes each token through a simple embedding matrix and SelfAtt encodes the sequence using BERT (Devlin et al., 2019). Feng et al. (2020) pre-trained a bi-modal (natural language and programming language) transformer encoder based on RoBERTa (Liu et al., 2019), with the hybrid objectives of Mask Language Model (MLM) and Replaced Token Detection (RTD). The model is then fine-tuned for the code search task on each programming language dataset. We refer readers to the original papers (Husain et al., 2019; Feng et al., 2020) for further model details and hyperparameters.

	Datapoints	Unique Docstrings			
		Total	*Training*	*Validation*	*Test*
Go	346 365	277 118	253 979	11 757	11 382
Java	496 688	372 894	340 380	11 621	20 893
JS	138 625	123 738	111 443	6 876	5 419
PHP	578 118	424 657	387 470	17 843	19 344
Python	457 461	421 263	379 864	20 897	20 502
Ruby	53 279	47 763	43 549	2 089	2 125
All	2 070 536	1 667 433	1 516 685	71 083	79 665

Table 1: Dataset Size Statistics.

4 Dataset and Pre-processing

In this section, we introduce the CodeSearchNet Dataset (Husain et al., 2019) used in this paper and the code specific pre-processing strategies (e.g., tokenization) to be compared.

4.1 Dataset

CodeSearchNet[2] is a proxy dataset prepared from non-fork open-source Github repositories. It consists of 2M docstring–code pairs and 4M unlabeled code fragments, where the code fragments are function-level snippets and their respective docstrings (if any) serve as substitutes for natural language queries. Under CodeSearchNet, there are two sub-datasets, namely CodeSearchNet Corpus and CodeSearchNet Challenge. The CodeSearchNet Corpus dataset uses 2M docstrings as automatically-labeled queries, whereas the CodeSearchNet Challenge dataset uses another 99 free-text queries that were manually judged.

In this work we conduct all experiments on the CodeSearchNet Corpus dataset. The labeled data are split into training, validation, and test sets in a ratio of 80:10:10. Table 1 shows the overall dataset size and the number of unique docstrings in each data split. The test set is partitioned into segments of size 1000 at the evaluation stage, and the correct code snippet for a given query is compared against the other snippets within the same segment. That is, the code snippets in the 1000 `<docstring, code snippet>` pairs naturally form the *distractor* set for each other.

4.2 De-duplication

According to Husain et al. (2019), the crawled data are filtered according to certain heuristic rules,

[2]`https://github.com/github/CodeSearchNet`

```
# Appends the given string at the end of
    the current string value for key k.
def putcat (k, v)
  k = k.to_s; v = v.to_s
  lib.abs_putcat(@db, k, Rufus::Tokyo.
    blen(k), v, Rufus::Tokyo.blen(v))
end

# Appends the given string at the end of
    the current string value for key k.
def putcat (k, v)
  k = k.to_s; v = v.to_s
  @db.putcat(k, v)
end
```

Figure 1: Docstring duplication example (unused docstring and extra blank lines are removed).

	Docstrings	Duplicates (Number / Fraction)			
		Total		*Same repo*	
Go	277 118	18 531	6.7%	15 255	82.3%
Java	372 894	39 067	10.5%	34 072	87.2%
JS	123 738	7 254	5.9%	3 342	46.1%
PHP	424 657	42 058	9.9%	23 515	55.9%
Python	421 263	20 776	4.9%	16 608	79.9%
Ruby	47 763	3 006	6.3%	2 499	83.1%
All	1 667 433	130 692	7.4%	95 291	72.9%

Table 2: Docstring Duplicate Statistics. The *Docstring* column is the same as the the *Unique Docstring* in Table 1. *Total* indicates the number and proportion of duplicate docstrings in each programming language across the *entire* dataset. *From Same Repo* indicates the number and proportion of docstrings whose duplicates are found *all* in the same repository.

including removing (1) pairs where the docstring is shorter than three tokens, (2) functions that contain fewer than three lines, contain the "test" substring, or serve as constructors or standard extension methods, and (3) duplicate functions. Nevertheless, even though duplicate functions are removed, queries prepared from docstrings can still repeat. That is, different functions can share the same documentation. Such duplication may result from function overloading, oversimplified documentation, or mere coincidence. An example of this duplication is shown in Figure 1.

Table 2 shows that such query duplication can be observed in all programming languages to some degree, and most of the duplication arises from functions in the same repository. Considering the number of duplicate docstrings, it is inaccurate to consider all functions other than the one matched to the current query as negative samples. In this work, we aggregate all functions sharing the same docstring and regard all of them as relevant results.

4.3 Pre-processing

In all experiments, we apply the Porter stemmer and perform stopword removal using the default stopwords list in the Anserini toolkit (Yang et al., 2017), which is a Lucene-based IR system.

On top of this default configuration, we investigate the effectiveness of the following tokenization and stopword removal strategies specific to programming languages:

- no-code-tokenization: No extra pre-processing is applied other than Porter stemmer and removal of English stopwords.
- code-tokenization: Tokens in both `camelCase` and `snake_case` in code snippets and documentation are further tokenized into separate tokens, e.g., `camel case` and `snake case`.[3]
- code-tokenization + remove reserved tokens: Considering that reserved tokens in programming languages intuitively add little value in exact match methods, we remove the reserved tokens of each programming language on top of the code-tokenization condition.

We show length and vocabulary statistics after applying each pre-processing strategy in Table 3. In the table, *total vocab size* is the number of tokens that appear in either docstring or code, and *overlapped vocabulary ratio* is the percentage of tokens appearing in both docstring and code in the entire vocabulary. The table shows that code tokenization greatly shrinks the vocabulary size and raises the overlapped vocabulary ratio. Interestingly, reserved token removal shortens the code snippets length, but shows little impact on the overall vocabulary size. This results from the fact that reserved tokens are commonly contained in variable names as subtokens and thus reappear after code tokenization (e.g., the variable name `class_dir` would be tokenized into `class` and `dir`, therefore `class` would still appear in the final vocabulary).

5 Experiments

5.1 Experimental Setup

All our experiments were conducted with Capreolus (Yates et al., 2020), an IR toolkit integrating ranking and reranking tasks under the same data

[3]According to Husain et al. (2019), NBoW and SelfAtt tokenize 'camelCase' tokens into subtokens ('camel' and 'case'), which is similar to our code-tokenization setting.

		Ruby	JS	Go	Python	Java	PHP
	avg docstring length	14	13	20	14	15	8
no-code-tokenization	**avg code length**	37	73	44	60	47	45
keep reserved tokens	**total vocab size**	160 175	455 771	651 143	1 255 725	1 248 229	1 061 762
	overlapped vocab %	13.58%	10.18%	33.02%	9.92%	8.02%	7.49%
	avg docstring len	15	13	24	14	16	8
code-tokenization	**avg code len**	57	110	64	88	85	72
keep reserved tokens	**total vocab size**	31 999	76 305	68 877	191 608	105 005	134 729
	overlapped vocab %	40.13%	28.24%	36.83%	26.41%	28.62%	21.34%
	avg docstring len	15	13	28	14	16	8
code-tokenization	**avg code len**	48	93	57	78	74	62
remove reserved tokens	**total vocab size**	31 999	76 305	68 877	191 608	105 004	134 729
	overlapped vocab %	40.12%	28.24%	36.83%	26.41%	28.62%	21.34%

Table 3: Average length and vocabulary statistics after applying each pre-processing strategy.

Models		Ruby	JS	Go	Python	Java	PHP
CodeBERT		0.6926	0.7059	0.8400	0.8685	0.7484	0.7062
NBoW		0.4285	0.4607	0.6409	0.5809	0.4835	0.5181
SelfAtt		0.3651	0.4506	0.6809	**0.6922**	0.5866	**0.6011**
no-code-tokenization + keep reserved tokens	BM25	0.4484	0.4097	0.6979	0.4317	0.4002	0.3758
	BM25+RM3	0.4427	0.4123	0.6761	0.4216	0.3988	0.4062
code-tokenization + keep reserved tokens	BM25	<u>**0.5789**</u>	<u>**0.5522**</u>	0.7289	<u>0.5989</u>	<u>**0.6022**</u>	<u>0.5929</u>
	BM25+RM3	0.5735	0.5312	0.7214	0.5865	0.5777	0.5379
code-tokenization + remove reserved tokens	BM25	0.5707	0.5312	<u>**0.7317**</u>	0.5905	0.5838	0.5399
	BM25+RM3	0.5703	0.5269	0.7246	0.5871	0.5794	0.5400

Table 4: MRR on the test set of the CodeSearchNet Corpus where each model searches for the correct code snippet against the 999 distractors. The highest scores among non-BERT models are highlighted in **bold**, and the ones among keyword-only models are <u>underlined</u>. We copied the scores of neural ranking models from Husain et al. (2019) and Feng et al. (2020).

processing pipeline. We chose the toolkit to enhance reproducibility and to support future comparisons. Note that although Capreolus is primarily designed for text ranking with neural ranking models, in this work we do not use any of those features. The underlying implementation of BM25 and RM3 are provided by the Pyserini toolkit (Lin et al., 2021), which in turn is built on the Lucene open-source search library, but Capreolus provides simplified mechanisms for parameter tuning and other useful features for end-to-end experiments.

Following the original paper (Husain et al., 2019), each correct code snippet was searched against a fixed set of 999 *distractors*, as described in Section 4.1. All experiments were evaluated with Mean Reciprocal Rank (MRR). In all experiments, we tuned the parameters `k1` and `b` for BM25 and `originalQueryWeight`, `fbDocs`, `fbTerms` for RM3 on the validation set, then applied the parameters from the best result on the test set. Note that since BM25 and RM3 only require parameter tuning, we did not use the training set mentioned in Table 1.

`k1`	[0.7, 1.3], step size 0.1
`b`	[0.7, 1.0], step size 0.1
`fbDocs`	[55, 95], step size 10
`fbTerms`	2, 5, 7, 10
`originalQueryWeight`	0.7, 0.8, 0.9

Table 5: BM25 and RM3 parameter values explored.

After pilot experiments on the Ruby and Go datasets to determine reasonable parameter ranges to search, we performed a grid search on each language dataset over the values shown in Table 5.

5.2 Results and Analysis

The results are shown in Table 4. The first row reports the results of CodeBERT (Feng et al., 2020). We list this result here to better compare the IR baselines with the state-of-the-art model in the field. The next two rows are pre-BERT neural model results copied from Husain et al. (2019). The remaining rows show the scores of BM25 and RM3 with the three aforementioned pre-processing strategies on the six programming language datasets.

As Table 4 shows, BM25 and BM25 + RM3 in general outperform the NBoW and SelfAtt baselines despite variations in effectiveness across programming languages. The SelfAtt model only shows sizeable improvement over BM25 on Python and a modest improvement on PHP. This suggests that the gap between natural language and programming languages does not necessarily hinder traditional IR methods in the code search task, and that distributed representations are not necessarily better at addressing this gap.

Comparing the results of BM25 and BM25 + RM3, we observe that adding RM3, which is generally considered more effective, does not improve over BM25 on any of the language datasets. We suspect the cause of this unanticipated result is that most of the queries in CodeSearchNet only have a single relevant document, which may not be sufficient to quantify the benefits of pseudo relevance feedback techniques. This hypothesis is supported by a similar observation that adding RM3 degrades effectiveness on the MS MARCO dataset (Bajaj et al., 2018), where each query also has few relevant documents (Lin et al., 2020).

The results from each pre-processing strategy show the necessity of code tokenization, which improves MRR overall. On the other hand, removing the reserved tokens does not improve effectiveness. The possible reasons could be that (1) some reserved tokens are in the English stopwords list and would be removed anyway (e.g. `for`, `if`, `or`, etc.), (2) some special reserved tokens rarely appear in the query and thus contribute little to the final score (e.g. `elif`, `await`, etc.), and (3) frequently-appearing reserved words are given small IDF weights in BM25, which minimizes their effect (e.g. `final`, `return`, `var`).

6 Conclusion

In this paper we examined the effectiveness of traditional IR methods for semantic code search and found that while these exact match methods are not as effective as CodeBERT, they generally outperform pre-BERT neural models. We also compare the effect of code-specific tokenization strategies, showing that while splitting camel and snake case is beneficial, removing reserved tokens does not necessarily help keyword-based methods.

There are also aspects of semantic code search that this paper does not cover. Sachdev et al. (2018) mentioned the nuance between different code components, such as how readability can differ for function names and local variables. We leave for future work an investigation of whether treating such components differently improves effectiveness. Nevertheless, the lesson from our work seems clear: even with advances in neural approaches, we shouldn't neglect comparisons to and contributions from strong keyword-based IR methods.

Acknowledgements

This research has been supported by the Natural Sciences and Engineering Research Council (NSERC) of Canada.

References

Nasreen Abdul-Jaleel, James Allan, W. Bruce Croft, Fernando Diaz, Leah Larkey, Xiaoyan Li, Donald Metzler, Mark D. Smucker, Trevor Strohman, Howard Turtle, and Courtney Wade. 2004. UMass at TREC 2004: Novelty and HARD. In *Proceedings of the Thirteenth Text REtrieval Conference (TREC 2004)*, Gaithersburg, Maryland.

Lakshmanan Arumugam. 2020. Semantic code search using Code2Vec: A bag-of-paths model. Master's thesis, University of Waterloo.

Payal Bajaj, Daniel Campos, Nick Craswell, Li Deng, Jianfeng Gao, Xiaodong Liu, Rangan Majumder, Andrew McNamara, Bhaskar Mitra, Tri Nguyen, Mir Rosenberg, Xia Song, Alina Stoica, Saurabh Tiwary, and Tong Wang. 2018. MS MARCO: A Human Generated MAchine Reading COmprehension Dataset. *arXiv:1611.09268v3*.

Jose Cambronero, Hongyu Li, Seohyun Kim, Koushik Sen, and Satish Chandra. 2019. When deep learning met code search. In *Proceedings of the 2019 27th ACM Joint Meeting on European Software Engineering Conference and Symposium on the Foundations of Software Engineering*, ESEC/FSE 2019, page 964–974, New York, NY, USA. Association for Computing Machinery.

Jacob Devlin, Ming-Wei Chang, Kenton Lee, and Kristina Toutanova. 2019. BERT: Pre-training of deep bidirectional transformers for language understanding. In *Proceedings of the 2019 Conference of the North American Chapter of the Association for Computational Linguistics: Human Language Technologies, Volume 1 (Long and Short Papers)*, pages 4171–4186, Minneapolis, Minnesota. Association for Computational Linguistics.

Zhangyin Feng, Daya Guo, Duyu Tang, Nan Duan, Xiaocheng Feng, Ming Gong, Linjun Shou, Bing Qin, Ting Liu, Daxin Jiang, and Ming Zhou. 2020. CodeBERT: A pre-trained model for programming and natural languages. In *Findings of the Association for Computational Linguistics: EMNLP 2020*, pages 1536–1547, Online. Association for Computational Linguistics.

Luyu Gao, Zhuyun Dai, Zhen Fan, and Jamie Callan. 2020. Complementing lexical retrieval with semantic residual embedding. *arXiv:2004.13969*.

Wenchao Gu, Zongjie Li, Cuiyun Gao, Chaozheng Wang, Hongyu Zhang, Zenglin Xu, and Michael R. Lyu. 2021. CRaDLe: Deep code retrieval based on semantic dependency learning. *Neural Networks*, 141:385–394.

Xiaodong Gu, Hongyu Zhang, and Sunghun Kim. 2018. Deep code search. In *Proceedings of the 40th International Conference on Software Engineering*, ICSE '18, page 933–944, New York, NY, USA. Association for Computing Machinery.

Daya Guo, Shuo Ren, Shuai Lu, Zhangyin Feng, Duyu Tang, Shujie Liu, L. Zhou, Nan Duan, Jian Yin, Daxin Jiang, and M. Zhou. 2020. GraphCodeBERT: Pre-training code representations with data flow. *arXiv:2009.08366*.

Hamel Husain, Ho-Hsiang Wu, Tiferet Gazit, Miltiadis Allamanis, and Marc Brockschmidt. 2019. CodeSearchNet Challenge: Evaluating the state of semantic code search. *arXiv:1909.09436*.

Victor Lavrenko and W. Bruce Croft. 2001. Relevance based language models. In *Proceedings of the 24th Annual International ACM SIGIR Conference on Research and Development in Information Retrieval*, SIGIR '01, page 120–127, New York, NY, USA. Association for Computing Machinery.

Jimmy Lin, Xueguang Ma, Sheng-Chieh Lin, Jheng-Hong Yang, Ronak Pradeep, and Rodrigo Nogueira. 2021. Pyserini: A Python toolkit for reproducible information retrieval research with sparse and dense representations. In *Proceedings of the 44th International ACM SIGIR Conference on Research and Development in Information Retrieval*, SIGIR'21, New York, NY, USA. Association for Computing Machinery.

Jimmy Lin, Rodrigo Nogueira, and Andrew Yates. 2020. Pretrained transformers for text ranking: BERT and beyond. *arXiv:2010.06467*.

Xiang Ling, Lingfei Wu, Saizhuo Wang, Gaoning Pan, Tengfei Ma, Fangli Xu, Alex X. Liu, Chunming Wu, and Shouling Ji. 2021. Deep graph matching and searching for semantic code retrieval. *ACM Transactions on Knowledge Discovery from Data*, 15(5):Article No. 88.

Y. Liu, Myle Ott, Naman Goyal, Jingfei Du, Mandar Joshi, Danqi Chen, Omer Levy, M. Lewis, Luke Zettlemoyer, and Veselin Stoyanov. 2019. RoBERTa: A robustly optimized BERT pretraining approach. *arXiv:1907.11692*.

Stephen Robertson and Hugo Zaragoza. 2009. The probabilistic relevance framework: BM25 and beyond. *Foundation and Trends in Information Retrieval*, 3(4):333–389.

Stephen E. Robertson and Karen Sparck Jones. 1976. Relevance weighting of search terms. *Journal of the American Society for Information science*, 27(3):129–146.

Saksham Sachdev, Hongyu Li, Sifei Luan, Seohyun Kim, Koushik Sen, and Satish Chandra. 2018. Retrieval on source code: A neural code search. In *Proceedings of the 2nd ACM SIGPLAN International Workshop on Machine Learning and Programming Languages*, MAPL 2018, page 31–41, New York, NY, USA. Association for Computing Machinery.

Kavitha Srinivas, I. Abdelaziz, Julian T. Dolby, and J. McCusker. 2020. Graph4Code: A machine interpretable knowledge graph for code. *arXiv:2002.09440*.

Zhensu Sun, Y. Liu, Chen Yang, and Yu Qian. 2020. PSCS: A path-based neural model for semantic code search. *arXiv:2008.03042*.

Peilin Yang, Hui Fang, and Jimmy Lin. 2017. Anserini: Enabling the use of Lucene for information retrieval research. In *Proceedings of the 40th International ACM SIGIR Conference on Research and Development in Information Retrieval*, SIGIR '17, page 1253–1256, New York, NY, USA. Association for Computing Machinery.

Wei Yang, Kuang Lu, Peilin Yang, and Jimmy Lin. 2019. Critically examining the "neural hype": Weak baselines and the additivity of effectiveness gains from neural ranking models. In *Proceedings of the 42nd International ACM SIGIR Conference on Research and Development in Information Retrieval*, SIGIR'19, page 1129–1132, New York, NY, USA. Association for Computing Machinery.

Andrew Yates, Kevin Martin Jose, Xinyu Zhang, and Jimmy Lin. 2020. Flexible IR pipelines with Capreolus. In *Proceedings of the 29th ACM International Conference on Information & Knowledge Management*, CIKM '20, page 3181–3188, New York, NY, USA. Association for Computing Machinery.

Qihao Zhu, Zeyu Sun, Xiran Liang, Yingfei Xiong, and Lu Zhang. 2020. OCoR: An overlapping-aware code retriever. In *Proceedings of the 35th IEEE/ACM International Conference on Automated Software Engineering*, ASE '20, page 883–894, New York, NY, USA. Association for Computing Machinery.

Author Index

Association for Computational Linguistics
209 N. Eighth Street
Stroudsburg, Pennsylvania 18360

ISBN 978-1-7138-3383-3

9 781713 833833

CURRAN ASSOCIATES INC.
proceedings.com